Mindfulness

Improve the Health of Your Mind, Body and Soul
Using Mindfulness Meditation

(Become More Aware of Your Senses for Extreme
Focus and Happiness)

Eric Gomez

Published by Rob Miles

© **Eric Gomez**

All Rights Reserved

Mindfulness: Improve the Health of Your Mind, Body and Soul Using Mindfulness Meditation (Become More Aware of Your Senses for Extreme Focus and Happiness)

ISBN 978-1-989990-85-8

All rights reserved. No part of this guide may be reproduced in any form without permission in writing from the publisher except in the case of brief quotations embodied in critical articles or reviews.

Legal & Disclaimer

The information contained in this book is not designed to replace or take the place of any form of medicine or professional medical advice. The information in this book has been provided for educational and entertainment purposes only.

The information contained in this book has been compiled from sources deemed reliable, and it is accurate to the best of the Author's knowledge; however, the Author cannot guarantee its accuracy and validity and cannot be held liable for any errors or omissions. Changes are periodically made to this book. You must consult your doctor or get professional medical advice before using any of the suggested remedies, techniques, or information in this book.

Upon using the information contained in this book, you agree to hold harmless the Author from and against any damages, costs, and expenses, including any legal fees potentially resulting from the application of any of the information provided by this guide. This disclaimer applies to any damages or injury caused by the use and application, whether directly or indirectly, of any advice or information presented, whether for breach of contract, tort, negligence, personal injury, criminal intent, or under any other cause of action.

You agree to accept all risks of using the information presented inside this book. You need to consult a professional medical practitioner in order to ensure you are both able and healthy enough to participate in this program.

Table of Contents

INTRODUCTION 1

CHAPTER 1: MINDFULNESS BASICS 4

CHAPTER 2: MINDFULNESS FOR CAREGIVERS 9

CHAPTER 3: WHAT IS MINDFULNESS? 20

CHAPTER 4: MINDFULNESS MEDITATION PRACTICE 32

CHAPTER 5: THE WORLD OF MINDFULNESS 38

CHAPTER 6: THE WAY TO MINDFULNESS 45

CHAPTER 7: WHAT IS BUDDHISM? 52

CHAPTER 8: BREAKING AUTOPILOT 65

CHAPTER 9: WHY AND HOW TO CONTROL YOUR EMOTIONS 74

CHAPTER 10: DISCOVERING MINDFULNESS 78

CHAPTER 11: MINDFULNESS-BASED STRESS REDUCTION 86

CHAPTER 12: MINDFUL BREATHING MEDITATION 101

CHAPTER 13: UNDERSTANDING STRESS 105

CHAPTER 14: EXPLORING THE TECHNIQUES AND PRINCIPLES OF MEDITATION 118

CHAPTER 15: ADOPTING MINDFULNESS AS A WAY OF LIFE 136

CHAPTER 16: TRACK YOUR SUCCESS AND IMPROVE YOUR TECHNIQUE 147

- CHAPTER 17: TAKE CARE OF YOURSELF 152
- CHAPTER 18: MY EXPERIENCE OF LIFE 154
- CHAPTER 19: WHAT IS MINDFULNESS? 160
- CHAPTER 20: HARNESSING THE PRESENT 164
- CHAPTER 21: UNDERSTANDING MINDFULNESS............. 170
- CHAPTER 22: WHAT IS THE PRACTICE OF MINDFULNESS? 177
- CHAPTER 23: WHAT IS MINDFULNESS? 185
- CHAPTER 24: WHAT IS MEDITATION?............................ 192
- CONCLUSION.. 203

Introduction

Since the 1970s, people who suffer from generalized anxiety disorder, stress, depression, psychosis, addiction, and other forms of mental disorder or psychological condition, have been advised to turn to clinical psychology and psychiatry. Efforts to provide succor to these sufferers made way for the development of several therapeutic applications.

Eventually, mindfulness came to be recognized as a therapeutic procedure that could help to prevent the above psychological conditions or to reduce their severity. For instance, the practice of mindfulness has been adopted as a preventive strategy to stop the development of various mental health issues.

In the Western world, Jon Kabat Zinn is generally accepted as the propagator of mindful meditation, and no contrary opinion has ever gained prominence. As one of its doctrines, Buddhism employs mindfulness to encourage self-knowledge and wisdom, which is believed to gradually lead to what the Buddhists call "enlightenment" and also describes total freedom from suffering.

Since the time of Zinn, "mindfulness" has become a field study that researchers have always sought to understand more. Together with Focus, Mindfulness is currently one of the hot topics in the communities of Leadership and Management, especially in the management of social and family issues. A lot of top and middle management mental health professionals are now asking various questions on this very topic of mindfulness.

Unfortunately, the efforts they have put into the search are not matched by the end results, chiefly because they're yet to come to the terms with where to begin. This eBook is specifically written to address this concern and the similar ones above. The challenges encountered in a bid to understand mindfulness by people from all walks of life, coupled with an active interest in adopting the practice inform the tones and language of this eBook.

In its three chapters, we try to put on the table the very essence of mindfulness. Mindfulness as a concept is defined in the first chapter, while chapter two tries to explain how mindfulness can make you happier than you are now and shows you how to achieve the actual mindful meditation. The third chapter takes a look at negative emotions, their impact, and how to manage them through mindfulness.

When people hear the word "mindfulness" they draw up different kinds of images—of people sitting in a special way, wearing some kind of special attire, and other pictures drawn from all the misconceived ideas out there. Interestingly enough, mindfulness is something that is rather obscure or mysterious, though it can be quite spiritual. Let's now attempt to define mindfulness as a whole.

Chapter 1: Mindfulness Basics

Our journey of stress relief begins with an understanding of some fundamentals of the practice of mindfulness. The discipline has its origins in Buddhism, but is also used by psychologists and psychiatrists to treat patients with different psychological conditions. Among the most common applications for mindfulness is stress reduction and stress prevention.

Mindfulness uses meditative techniques to focus one's attention on the events occurring in this very moment. Special attention is paid to the individual's feelings, both physical and emotional, as well as thoughts. Two essential facets of mindfulness are acceptance and non-judgmental thoughts.

You may have heard mindfulness referred to as living in the moment. That's the exact intent. Rather than fleeing the moment, practitioners of mindfulness embrace and explore the moment to better understand their own feelings and reactions.

Mindful meditations take us away from our concentration on negative emotions and free us to inhabit the present fully. Fear and anxiety are the two emotions that rob us of our ability to inhabit the present. Fear in the present stems from anxiety about what happened in the past or what we think will happen to us in the future.

Let's use an example. I'll use my own experience to illustrate that literally anyone can learn these techniques. In a previous profession, I had to roll up reports to corporate executives from the team I managed every Thursday by the close of business. I never felt stress on Thursdays as I calmly processed the reports and submitted them.

However, the following week in advance of our staff meeting, I always felt stressed. The stress was an echo of the previous week's report, because I felt anxious about how well the information had been received. When I realized my stress was not caused by the staff meeting, I was able to understand how to correctly identify and manage my feelings of anxiety.

That's the power an individual taps into through the practice of mindfulness. By narrowing our focus, we can alleviate stress, anxiety and fear. Mindfulness is also connected with effective treatments for substance abuse as well as other addictive or habitual patterns.

The results and effectiveness of mindfulness exercises have been demonstrated across several psychological studies. In many instances the effects were shown to match or exceed the effects of prescription medication for relief of stress, anxiety and depression.

Mindfulness is essential in reducing work-related stresses. Studies are showing stress is rapidly becoming the most common workplace addiction. What we do to focus on the moment will enable us to be more productive, shoo away stressors and find our work to be more rewarding and satisfying.

How you approach the practice of mindfulness is entirely up to you. You may find it applies to many areas of your life. You may prefer to keep it as a handy tool to cope with and prevent workplace stress. I personally have found its application in my professional life to be as important as how I use mindfulness in my personal life.

These strategies and techniques are just a guide. If you find yourself feeling extremely stressed multiple times a day, as in the 8s, 9s, and 10s from the list we made in the Introduction, you will definitely benefit from these exercises. However, you should also consider the benefits you might derive from visiting with a behavioral health professional. A professional can take the basic exercises presented in this book and amplify their effectiveness through cognitive behavioral therapy or dialectical behavioral therapy. As always, the choice of best treatments for your particular situation is up to you.

Before we move on to the exercises in Chapter 2, I wanted to ask you to pull your journal back out, or the scratchpad where you made your columns with the various stressors you feel on the job. Look at the stressor that creates within you the strongest reaction. I want you to underline it. We're going to focus our attention on that particular stressor to help you cope better.

In addition, I'll tell you what my biggest workplace stress was. I had a very aggressive and overbearing supervisor at a previous job. His demeanor was so harsh that I literally found my heart rate elevated just by the sound of his voice. Interacting with him was consistently a 9. I'll share how I got it down to a 2 as we go through the book. Once you made your selection, we'll move onto Chapter 2.

Chapter 2: Mindfulness For Caregivers

The people who surround someone with an injury or illness can also benefit from mindfulness, because they are affected by a loved one's illness or injury too. New research is being done that shows people who take care of or live with someone who has PTSD or Depression can start to show the same symptoms from the stress and anxiety of living with and caring for someone with PTSD or Depression.

Many military spouses are being diagnosed with Secondary Post Traumatic Stress because of the anxiety and stress caused by caring for a service member that has PTSD. Caregivers of those with PTSD and Depression will start to show symptoms like hyper-vigilance, hyper-sensitivity, avoidance, fear and anxiety. Taking care of yourself by practicing mindfulness will not only protect you, it will help you be strong enough to help your loved one that is struggling or needs your care.

Mindful Meditation

Most of the time we walk around in a fog of nonstop thoughts that makes it very difficult to live mindfully. When you are walking on the street you are probably thinking about work, or your family, or that video you saw online, or the coffee you are going to get but not about the trees around you or the sunlight on your face or the air that you're breathing.

There are many ways that you can practice mindfulness throughout the day. When people talk about mindfulness usually they are referring to mindful meditation. Mindful meditation is a specific type of meditation that is excellent for relieving stress and anxiety.

Mindful meditation, which focuses on breathing, can be performed during a scheduled meditation session or in a moment of panic or anxiety in order to regain focus and control and a feeling of safety. Mindful meditation is a powerful tool for people that suffer from anxiety and Depression.

Becoming more mindful is something that will transform your life. When you are more aware of your own emotions and your own abilities you will be able to see a future for yourself that you may never have seen before. Mindfulness will keep you connected to yourself and integrate your body and mind.

Being more mindful is something that you can learn with very little effort. At the core being mindful is imply paying attention without judgment. Detach, observe, and stay connected to yourself the world by recognizing that you are part of the world but you are not the center of it.

Mindful meditation and living mindfully are more important in modern culture than they ever were before. Because our lives now are lived online through computers and smart phone and tablets it can be difficult to disconnect, step back, and be fully present. Learning to disconnect in a mindful way can have enormous physical and emotional benefits.

Myths about Mindful Meditation

Before we go over how to meditate mindfully let's take a quick look at some of the myths associated with mindful meditation. Over the years mindful meditation has gotten lumped in with some New Age practices that make people doubt whether or not meditation is really effective. Here are a few of the myths about mindful meditation that you may have heard before:

Meditation is New Age Hooey

This is a myth that a lot of people believe even though it's been scientifically proven to be false. Mindful meditation is an ancient practice that has survived for thousands of years because it works. Science has proven repeatedly that meditation has a dramatic effect on the body. An MRI scan of the brain during meditation shows how the brain will slow down and how the body relaxes during meditation. Meditation works, and it can work for anyone. (Guide, 2014)

You Can't be a Christian and Meditate

Meditation is a totally secular practice. Even though it stems from Buddhism you don't need to be a Buddhist to meditate. You can practice whatever faith you want to practice or no faith at all. It doesn't make any difference when you are meditating. In fact, many religions encourage meditation as a way to enter a prayerful state and connect with the Divine.

You Need to Spend Hours Meditating

Just because the Buddhist monks spend hours meditating doesn't mean that you need to in order to get the benefits of meditation. Mindful meditation can be done in as little as five minutes. If you have an hour and you want to meditate for an hour you can, but if you're panicking and you are using mindful meditation to calm yourself down you don't have to meditate for an hour before you will feel calmer. You will calmer in just a few minutes of focused breathing.

You Need Special Equipment to Meditate

You may have put off learning mindful meditation because you think that you need special equipment like candles and incense in order to meditate. That's just not true. You can meditate anywhere, at any time. Some people do like to use tools like fountains, candles or incense to help them meditate but none of things are necessary to meditate. Some people like to listen to guided meditations on an MP3 player or on a smart phone to help them focus. If you choose to use tools that is up to you but it's not something you need to do.

You Need a Special Meditation Room

When most people think of meditation they think of a quiet room, empty except for a mat or cushion on the floor, and they think that they can't meditate if they don't have a huge room to devote to meditation. Some people do like to meditate in a certain room but the truth is that you can meditate anywhere, and at any time.

You can meditate at your desk, or in your car. You can meditate while you are shopping or while you are in the shower. There is no rule that you have to have an entire room set aside just for meditation. You don't even need to meditate indoors.

The only requirement for meditation is that you be in a place where you can shut your eyes for a few moments and relax.

Meditation is Trying to Escape From Problems

In fact, the opposite of this is true. Meditation isn't trying to escape from your problems or minimize your problems. Mindful meditation is facing your problems head on. It is looking at the situation that you are in right now and accepting it, not judging it. Simple observing the situation that you are in and feeling your feelings about it.

It can be very difficult to look at your circumstances without any judgment. You may want to blame the person that caused the accident, blame a higher power for allowing you to become injured, or blame the people that are causing stress in your life. But blame and regret don't solve problems or open up new doorways for you. Meditation can give you the vision that you need to see new paths that are unfolding in front of you.

It's only after you take an honest assessment of where you are at right now that you can move forward. Mindful meditation is the act of examining yourself and your situation without judgment, blame, or other emotions clouding the situation. Once you know exactly where you are then you can start to move forward.

A 3-Step Approach to Practice Mindful Meditation

Mindful meditation isn't that difficult. There are just three steps to it. The trick to mindful meditation is to maintain awareness, and to keep going. You don't need to spend hours meditating, although you certainly can if you have the time. Here are the three steps to mindful meditation:

Get Comfortable

You don't need to sit in any particular way in order to meditate. Just make sure that you are sitting or lying down with your back straight. That's the only requirement. Lay down on the couch if you want, or your bed. Sit in your chair at your desk. Or sit on the floor with your legs crossed. However you are comfortable is how you should be as long as your back is straight. And don't fall asleep.

Pay Attention to Your Breath

Where do you breathe from? Some people breathe from the nose, some people breathe from the mouth, others breathe deep from the belly. When you are meditating you don't need to change your breathing in any way. Just be aware of where your breath is coming from.

Close your eyes and pay attention to your breathing. Don't think about the project that is due later today or the stupid thing you said to your spouse or at your child's soccer game. Just think about your breath. Be aware of the sensations in your body as your breath travels into your lungs and out again.

Corral Your Thoughts

While you are focusing on your breathing your mind will wander. And that's ok. You may start thinking about strange things like your favorite meal when you were a child or what color scarf your neighbor wore to the last school play. Let your thoughts wander.

Just gather them up when you notice them wander away and bring them back to your conscious mind. Think about your breathing again and focus on your breath. After a few breaths bring your wandering thoughts back to your breath. Keep doing that as often as you need to.

And that's it! That's all there is to mindful meditation. The more you practice this the more it will become a habit and the easier it will be to drop into a mindful state. As you practice more and more mindful meditation you also will start to incorporate mindfulness into other areas of your life.

Mindful meditation is one of the most powerful tools that there is when you are fighting anxiety, Depression, fear, and pain. If you are willing to work at staying present and focusing your thoughts you can defeat these debilitating conditions and take control of your life.

You can start practicing mindful meditation right now. You don't need to wait for a certain time or wait until you are in the mood. Just sit up straight wherever you are reading this book. Shut your eyes. Focus on your breathing. Let your thoughts go wherever they want. Just keep bringing them back to focus on your breath over and over. You will immediately notice that you are calmer and more focused when you open your eyes again.

Chapter 3: What Is Mindfulness?

Mindfulness is giving your full attention to the present moment. All of your attention is focused on this moment, not on the past or future. It means being awake to life, as it is really occurring, and not judging or thinking about it. Just experiencing it. For practical purposes, the word mindfulness is being used to indicate the state of being fully attentive in the present moment. In reality, when you are completely alert in the present moment, your mind is not really "full". The state of being fully alert in the present moment is more accurately described as "mind-lessness", in which the mind is not full of thoughts, but instead the thinking mind is less active, just aware, with less thoughts.

For most people, their mind is almost always thinking. Their attention is hijacked by thoughts about the past (what has already happened), and thoughts about the future (what is going to happen). Most people think they think their own thoughts, but in reality, thinking is happening to them. If you were really in control of your own thoughts, would you ever have unpleasant thoughts? The fact that most human beings constantly think about negative things indicates that they are not actually thinking their own thoughts, but thinking is happening to them.

The goal is to be able to be so focused that you are able to think at will, and that you create some space between you and your thoughts so that when thoughts happen to you, you are able to bring your attention back to the present moment and not spiral downward. You can do this by paying attention to the present moment in order to interrupt the stream of unpleasant thoughts. You can't be thinking about the past or future and be fully present in the moment at the same time. By practicing mindfulness, you will begin to use your mind in a very powerful way instead of being a victim of the incessant negative thoughts that plague you right now.

Mindfulness is about living your life moment by moment, as if it really mattered. Most of the time we're not paying attention to what's happening right now.

•Pay close attention to your breathing, especially when you're feeling intense emotions.

•Notice the sights, sounds, and smells in this moment, bring them to your conscious awareness.

•Recognize that your thoughts and emotions are fleeting and do not define you, an insight that can free you from negative thought patterns.

•Tune into your body's physical sensations, from the water hitting your skin in the shower to the way your body rests in your office chair.

Why is mindfulness so hard?

Mindfulness can seem so hard because it feels like as soon as you become present thinking almost immediately resumes...so it feels like you never stop thinking. Living a truly present life is a skill that you learn, so the key is to keep bringing yourself back to the present moment. Your mind might be so active that it feels like for every 60 seconds you have to bring yourself back 55 times. If that's the case, stay with it. Over time, you will notice that the gaps between thoughts become longer. You will eventually get to a point where you can stop thinking at will. A lot of people get discouraged and say mindfulness doesn't work for them. It only doesn't work if you stop doing it.

Present Moment Reality Check

On a scale from 1 to 10, how at peace and at ease are you right now? If it's not at a 9 or a 10, ask yourself what keeps it from being higher?

Look around the room. What is actually happening? You might be sitting in a chair. You may have comfortable clothes on, sitting in a comfortable room. You probably ate today and have a roof over your head. Probably nobody is kicking you right now and nothing unpleasant is happening to you right now.

Is anything wrong right now? Do you have any problems right now? Your mind might begin to argue that yes, you have lots of problems. If you just focus on your actual experience in the present moment (reality), not on thoughts (non-reality), you'll notice that you don't have any problems right now. If you stay focused on the reality of this present moment, can the number go up at all? Most of the time you should be at a 9 or a 10. There will be times when this is not possible, but this should be very rare, like when you've experienced the loss of someone close to you. Even when challenging situations arise, you can still remain in a state of peace.

Your mind might be arguing that there's no way you can be at a 9 or 10 most of the time. Why do you think this is? Some people become so used to their negative thoughts and unhappiness that they can't even imagine they could be happy. It almost seems 'wrong' to be happy. Some people are actually addicted to their suffering. Seriously consider the actual reasons why you can't be at a 9 or 10 right now or most of the time.

How to know if you have unresolved issues

When you do a present moment reality check and you're not at a 10, then ask yourself what keeps you from being at a 10. Your answer may be: I feel anxious, or I feel sad. Ask yourself what you're anxious about, what you're sad about. If you don't know, ask yourself the first time you remember feeling that way. Whatever comes up is the starting point for healing the unresolved issue.

Stay Here

A powerful exercise for practicing present moment awareness is to silently repeat to yourself 'stay here', 'stay here'. Throughout the day, remind yourself to stay here as your thoughts attempt to sweep you away from reality, away from the present moment, away from life itself. Keep reminding yourself to stay here. Commit to being fully alive by staying here, by being attentive to the present moment, the only moment in which you are actually alive.

You are not your thoughts

You are not your thoughts. You have thoughts, but you are not your thoughts. This is a very important point because what makes some thoughts so distressing is that we identify with the thoughts. Being identified with thoughts means that your identity, or sense of self, is attached to the thought. If the thought comes up that "I'm unlovable" and I believe it's true, my actions will reflect the beliefs of someone who is unlovable. Begin dis-identifying with your thoughts by telling yourself "I don't have to believe everything that I think". Take the judgment out of it.

Instead of focusing on right and wrong and on whose fault it is, just ask yourself "does this work for me?" If it doesn't work for you, drop it. This takes courage. You will often find that honoring your truth means not making other people happy or not looking good in the eyes of others.

Your mind might argue with a lot of the information presented in order to keep you in a state of unhappiness. It will trick you into thinking that this is not useful or that it doesn't work for you. Just notice the thoughts and remain alert and present.

"When you run after your thoughts, you are like a dog chasing a stick: every time a stick is thrown, you run after it. Instead, be like a lion who, rather than chasing after the stick, turns to face the thrower. One only throws a stick at a lion once. " ~ Milarepa

Who are you, really?

There is a "you" that exists, that consists of your identity. For the purposes of this conversation, I will propose that there's the 'real' you and there's the 'you' created by thoughts, opinions, life experiences, social conditioning, etc. Let's call that the conceptualized you.

The real you is the you that's been there from the very start, when your little heartbeat started in your mother's womb. There was a life form, and it became 'you'. The real you is the part of you that is aware of what you have lived through. It's the awareness in the background that remains constant, never-changing, just there.

The conceptualized you that was created includes the name you were given, the values and morals you were taught, the personality you developed, the thoughts, beliefs and opinions you hold, the interests you became involved in, and much more. These are things you were not born with. Your body is part of you, but it is always changing. It does not look anything like what it was when you were 5 years old. Your body completely regenerates every 7 years, so physiologically you are not the same person (body) moment by moment.

Identity

A Transcendent Identity

The 'conceptualized self' (the self that people think they are) has many shortcomings and it causes a lot of fear and anxiety. When you think of 'yourself', it probably brings up a lot of negative thoughts about what you need to fix about yourself. Your mind says 'you' are a problem that needs to be fixed and that once your fix your shortcomings, you'll be happy. But this isn't true. Once you fix one thing, you notice something else that isn't good enough.

Transcendent means it transcends the person, going beyond the conceptualized self. On the surface level, every person has shortcomings. Become compassionate towards yourself, seeing that you are much more than your shortcomings. The shortcomings become less dysfunctional and cause less suffering the more you keep your attention on the deeper part of you, the 'real' you.

Perfection, or getting to the point in which a person has no more work to do on themselves and can't grow or evolve anymore isn't possible for human beings. There will always be opportunities to grow, things to learn, things that can be improved. The deeper you, the conscious you, is already perfect and complete. You don't need anything in order to become complete.

True identity vs conceptualized identity

The conceptualized identity includes a lot of negative, fearful thoughts which end up making us feel insecure, anxious, and afraid. Thought in itself is not problematic. Emotion is not problematic. Identification with thought and identification with emotion is problematic. When you become identified with thoughts it means the awareness behind the thoughts has been overshadowed so you get swept away by those thoughts and emotions. In those moments you act as if you ARE the thoughts instead of have thoughts.

The goal is to notice the thoughts but not to become identified with the thoughts (or emotions). This is not suppressing or denying, but just not becoming identified with it.

Staying present during an interaction is a vital skill. Don't become identified with what you are saying. Notice that what you are saying are just verbalized thoughts, and the key to presence is to not be identified with thinking. If you free your mind from identifications, your mind becomes a miracle.

Chapter 4: Mindfulness Meditation Practice

To get the full benefits of mindfulness practice, you need to practice informal practices of mindfulness alongside formal practices of mindfulness. Let's discuss the practices:

Sitting Meditation

Sitting meditation is one of the most effective practice of mindfulness. But remember, as the name suggests, the practice is not all about sitting down and closing your eyes. The practice:

Find the Spot: Find a place or spot in your house that is quiet and you will not be disturbed for at least 10-20 minutes. You can light a candle to create an atmosphere, according to your need.

Set correctly: Seat comfortably in a place that is stable and does not move around because of the weight of your body. You can simply sit on a folded blanket or on a cushion or you can choose a chair. If you choose a chair, make sure the chair has a flat seat and does not move too much towards the back. Make sure that your feet are not dangling on the floor, if needed, place something for support.

Check your posture: Make sure that your sitting posture is upright, but not too rigid of stiff. You can cross your legs in front of you if you are sitting on a cushion, just keep your hips higher than your knees. You can close your eyes or you can stare at the wall if it is close to you.

Be conscious of your environment and your body: Once you have settled yourself, try to be conscious of the environment you find yourself in. Stay as you are for a few minutes, remain conscious of the environment and the posture you find yourself. You will notice that your mind will wander off during this time; observe where it went and then bring your mind back to the environment that you find yourself and your body.

Breathing: Now start to focus on your breathing. Don't try to change how you breathe, just breathe normally. When practicing, don't try to alter your breathing pattern, just breathe as naturally as possible. Simply be conscious of your breathing process, allow your attention to rest on the breathing of yours. Notice how your breath goes in and the manner in which it comes out. While you are focusing on your breathing, don't forget about your body and the environment it is in.

Observe: Observe what is happening with you. You will notice that there are various thoughts that enter your mind; the thought might be about the movie you watched the other day or upcoming Summer vacation. Notice all your thoughts that enter your mind, without judging them or analyzing them. Then go to your breathing and the awareness of your environment and the body. If you are able to finish this process successfully, then you have finished your first mindfulness practice and give yourself credit for it. Make sure your practice sessions last for at least ten to twenty minutes.

Make it a ritual: Practice the sitting meditation daily. There is no fixed time frame for practicing. After a couple of weeks of practice, you can extend the practice session from 10-20 minutes to 20-30 minutes. The important thing is to practice daily.

Walking Meditation

For some of us, sitting in one place and practicing mindfulness is a dull and boring proposition. The walking meditation is the right practice for them. It may seem that walking and meditating is two different things and can't be done, but the walking meditation is the most powerful technique where is come to mediate. Let's discuss how you can walk and meditate at the same time. The practice:

Find a path: Choose a path that is helpful for your walking meditation. Choose one that is minimum thirty to forty feet long, where you can pace back and forth without anyone disturbing you.

Stand: Stand and be conscious of the process and focus on your balance. Make sure when you stand correctly and you are properly balanced. Try to feel things like the weight of your body on the surface of the earth and the way your feet connect into the ground underneath.

Walk: Start walking, don't try to change your usual style of walking. Just walk normally.

Awareness: You were conscious of your environment and your body when practicing sitting meditation. Similarly, when practicing walking mindfulness, let yourself be aware of all the finer nuances of walking. Be aware of the alternating patterns of contact and release of your feet as you walk. Notice your heel first touching the ground and then you are rolling over to the ball before it goes up into the air. While your feet are moving up and down, try to feel the sensation in your ankles. Focus on the feelings inside your shoes and the fabric of your socks. Be aware of any other feeling that you might have on your knees, shins, calves, hips and muscles. Beside this you want to be aware of any other parts of your body that might be affected by the walking; how your shoulders move when you walk, the way your chest makes contact with your clothing, and the feeling of air coursing over your hands as they move in the air. Don't allow yourself to get caught up in anything that might be passing your way or don't stare at anything.

Observe: Simply observe any distracting thought, feelings or emotional states that you might be facing. For example, if you are feeling low, then just observe the low feeling without trying to change it or thinking how you can get yourself into a happier state. Just observe your other thoughts and then return your attention to your walking meditation.

Stop: When you want to end your walking meditation, stop your walking naturally and avoid getting freeze at once.

Repeat: Practice the walking meditation 20 minutes daily.

Chapter 5: The World Of Mindfulness

From the moment that we wake up in the morning, to the last conscious thought at night, we are always thinking, planning, deciding and acting.

We are planning for the future that has not yet arrived, pondering on the past even though we cannot really change anything about it. We watch television and check our mail at the same time; we cook and listen to music simultaneously; we play with our children but keep our ears open for the 'ping' of the oven.

We read books and make 'to-do' lists at the same time; we drive and listen to our favorite books; we read digital versions of a book while commuting. Do you think we can really reach the depths of what our favorite authors are really trying to say when we are, at the same time, worrying around not running into another car in the road or reaching our station? We may be reading the words of the book, but we certainly don't understand what they are trying to tell us.

When we are doing multiple jobs at the same time, immersed in multiple thoughts and worries - not once are we fully concentrating on the job at hand; moreover, we are always focusing on more than our minds can handle.

In between preparing for the unforeseeable future and brooding about the unalterable past, when do you think we are living in the present?

The answer is: we are not. We are not really living in the moment, not in any moment of our life. The truth is, we are always too busy to live. Yes, we are breathing, eating and sleeping. We are eating gourmet food and travelling to exotic locations, watching mind blowing movies and reading thought provoking books, but we are still not living completely. Not in the actual sense, at least.

We are always saying that the best things in life are for free. But how many of us actually take the time to slow down and enjoy these beautiful moments of life? How many of us actually stop in our tracks to appreciate a newly-bloomed flower on the way to office instead of checking our emails? How many of us actually sit back and enjoy the sunset instead of watching the latest action-packed 3D movies on TV? When was the last time we have taken an hour-long nap, and woken up refreshed and satisfied, instead of worrying about the time that we wasted by sleeping?

We are almost always in a state of mindlessness - as opposed to mindfulness, which is the topic for this book - a state that makes us breeze through life without really living it. We are always in a hurry, in a rush, trying to catch life before we miss any single moment; but in this struggle, we are losing connection with the present - with the moment that we are living in.

That is where the art of mindfulness comes into context.

What is Mindfulness?

Mindfulness is the art of living in the present - a practice that we have long forgotten. It is the art of living in the moment, completely, focusing both our conscious and subconscious mind to the thoughts, actions and feelings that a person is experiencing in that precise moment.

By formal definition, mindfulness is,

"the intentional, accepting and non-judgmental focus of one's attention on the emotions, thoughts and sensations occurring in the present moment."

- wikipedia.com

Mindfulness is a state where you, as a person, are paying complete attention to the present, i.e. the moment that you are in. You are observing and experiencing every little thoughts and emotions that are coming to your mind. Instead of letting your life go by while you are busy trying to live, you are actually living.

Concentration, Mindfulness & Meditation

There are two common confusions that many have about mindfulness – one, which essential difference is there between mindfulness and concentration and 2. Is there any difference between mindfulness and meditation?

While practicing mindfulness it is important to know the difference between concentration and mindfulness. Concentration happens for a situation; it helps in focusing your mind on one thing or another letting you to take control of what goes on in your mind. Concentration is a tool helping you to be attentive. On the other hand mindfulness is a state – a constant state of alertness without where you have your mind present. This is a state you acquire through effort and time and through meditation.

Mindfulness is gained through meditation - yet it differs from its other forms. Meditation in general focuses on relaxation, freeing the mind from worries and filling it with peaceful thoughts. And mindfulness as a form of meditation stresses on process than outcome. Its intention is to focus more on the sensation of the body and to see what the mind does without focusing much on what it brings – process becomes more important than outcome and that is how one remains in the present.

History and Origin of Mindfulness

The modern term 'mindfulness' has its root into the Pali word 'sati' and the Sanskrit word 'smrti' - both of which roughly translates as 'to remember', giving us the initial idea of what mindfulness is about.

The concept of mindfulness was originally used by the Brahmins, the highest of Hindu castes, in memorizing Vedic Scriptures. From Hinduism, the notion of mindfulness was adopted by The Buddha, who used both the words 'sati' and 'smrti' in meditation.

From the eastern world, mindfulness was developed for the western world by Jon Kabat-Zinn and his colleagues at the University of Massachusetts Medical School to treat people with mental illnesses. They developed the Mindfulness-based Stress Reduction technique, or the MBSR technique, in 1979 focusing on helping people to respond effectively to stress, pressure and pain.

In the late 1990s, Professors Mark Williams and Zindel Segal and Dr. John

Teasdale took the notion of mindfulness further and developed the mindfulness-based Cognitive Therapy, or MBCT, to treat depression.

Today, mindfulness is a popular meditation technique that is being taught and practiced, and gaining fast popularity all over the world. In this complete guide to mindfulness, we will learn of ways that mindfulness can help us, and how we can learn important mindfulness exercises to implement in our everyday lives.

Chapter 6: The Way To Mindfulness

The Way to Mindfulness
There are many disciplines and practices that allow us to cultivate our mindfulness. These include meditation, yoga, tai chi, and qigong. These are all great methods. You should try a few of these out and decide which will work best for you.

There are a couple main forms of meditation along with some others that focus on different areas we want to work on.

1. Mindful Meditation - A form of meditation where you allow your attention and awareness to be open to all thoughts, sensations, sounds, feelings, images, and smells without evaluating or judging.

2. Concentration Meditation - A form of meditation where you try to narrow your focus and attention on your breath and a sound, image, or object. This will help to calm down your mind and let clarity and awareness come to the forefront.

Other Meditation Techniques

1. Transcendental Meditation (TM) - A popular and heavily researched form of meditation. This is a 7-step program that teaches using a sound or personal mantra to meditate while closing your eyes in a seated technique.

2. Loving Kindness Meditation - This form of meditation practices expressing a heartfelt wish of health and happiness to you and all the people in your life. This technique is used to cultivate the emotions of compassion, kindness, love, and appreciation.

3. Passage Meditation - This form of meditation makes use of the spiritual and inspirational passages that are backed by seven disciplines. The seven disciplines fit in with all religious and non-religious philosophy. This meditation allows the person practicing to remain focused, calm, and kind.

4. Awareness Meditation - This form of meditation practices observing our surroundings on a moment to moment basis. It teaches us to see the world as it

truly is. This meditation allows us to reach a clear and stable awareness of our thoughts without being weighed down by judgment.

5. Insight Meditation (Vipassana) - This form of meditation practices turning on a light so we can understand the subtle workings of our mind. Through the practice of mindfulness this meditation allows us to bring the real nature of our reality into better focus. It gives us a deep connection between our body and our mind.

6. Japa Meditation - This form of meditation practices repeating a Sanskrit mantra or term while using the rotation of a beaded Mala or rosary. This is an ideal form of meditation for people dealing with high levels of stress and tension.

7. Qigong & Tai Chi - This form of meditation is ideal for people who are passionate about martial arts and want to learn new relaxation and meditation techniques. This is often practiced among seniors as a form of both meditation and low impact exercise.

8. Yoga - A widely popular form of exercise with meditative benefits. This can be considered a movement meditation. It uses breathing and different relaxation poses to reduce the tension and stress from your body and mind. Yoga also provides an excellent workout and many physical health benefits.

9. Walking Meditations - This is one of my favorite meditative practices. I can fit a walk in everyday. I will sometimes listen to audio meditations while walking or will meditate on my own. Low impact and a great way to relieve stress after a long day.

Introductory Meditation Techniques

Many forms of meditation originated from a religious origin. That doesn't mean you need to be religious to enjoy the benefits meditation offers. The form of meditation you practice will depend on your preference. I enjoy yoga and walking meditations but I have many friends who swear by transcendental meditation.

Here are a few easy ways you can open your mind and learn to meditate. These are simple things you can do to start training your mind. They can all be done during your daily life. The purpose behind these techniques is to learn how to calm your mind and slow down. Once you've gotten good at both things, you'll be ready to move on to more advanced techniques.

Guided or Audio Meditation

You can find a calm, peace of mind while doing normal daily activities. Things that are routine can become mindfulness exercises you practice for deeper awareness and relaxation. I turned my walking and painting into an opportunity to practice my audio meditations. You could also do these while completing chores, running errands, swimming, or gardening.

Guided meditations are a form of meditation that uses stories, instruction, imagery, music, and natural sound effects to help you relax, focus, and follow along. Guided meditations come in many formats. Those include MP3, DVD, cassette tapes, and compact disc.

Another way to start meditating is finding relaxing activities when you start feeling stressed. Writing, reading, or listening to music are a few examples. These activities help to keep your mind focused while also lowering the level of your beta brain activity. This means your mind naturally eases into a deeper meditative state.

Brain Wave Entrainment is a form of audio meditation. It involves listening to an audio compact disc that uses binaural beats to help synchronize your brain waves and alter your brain wave frequency into a different state of being. This allows the person listening to get to a meditative state quicker.

Breath Awareness Meditation

Sit in an upright relaxed position. Keep your spine straight. Close your eyes and take a moment to be one with yourself. Be aware of the moment and what is happening, without taking action on any of it.

Once you're settled, notice your breath as it enters and leaves your body. Don't attempt to manipulate your breathing. Experience each breath and feel how the air goes in and out of your nose.

Experience how your body naturally moves when you breathe.

Your mind will wander. It will fall out of sync with your breath. This is a natural occurrence and not something to be concerned about. It's part of this meditation. You'll notice you're not only observing your breath, you are able to focus your attention back to your breath when your mind begins to wander.

Allow each of your emotions, experiences, bodily sensations, and thoughts to come and go while remaining in the background aware of your breath. Notice how each of these things come and goes, automatically and effortlessly like your breath.

As you gain experience, you'll discover the many tendencies your mind is capable of. You'll notice how your mind tries to resist and hold on to specific experiences. Allowing your mind to settle itself naturally will let you recognize these tendencies while allowing you the opportunity to let them go and all the negativity that is attached to them.

Chapter 7: What Is Buddhism?

Buddhism, widely perceived as the teachings of the great revolutionist Gautama (Shakyamuni) Buddha, or The Great Gautama, provides the world with a complete instruction of life – how it should rightly be lived, and why it should be lived like such. Buddhism is to be accepted as the first great revolution in the construction of life that differed from the common Godly religions.

That is not to say, however, that Buddhism was the first of this kind – there were many attempts to construct the means of life before his time, but none of which held their strength through the ages. Buddhism has lasted through the millenniums and thus the teachings of the Great Gautama are considered to be the first teachings of the laws of matter; the first teachings of the perfect construction of life itself.

Buddhism, then, is essentially the practice of the teachings of The Great Gautama, also known as 'Dharma', translating to 'protection'. In the practice of his great teachings, living beings shall be protected from suffering in every sense and interpretation of the word. Buddha demonstrated to the people our ultimate goal as living beings – enlightenment, or more so, the attainment of enlightenment. It is said that Buddha himself taught 84,000 teachings and, from this, the practice of Buddhism was born and developed in to what it is in the present day.

Today, we see many different forms of Buddhism, all of which stem from the teachings of the Great Gautama. For example, you may be familiar with Zen Buddhism and Theravada Buddhism. Regardless of which practice of Buddhism takes place, all teachings are precious – they are purely different presentations of the same, equally precious teachings.

Buddhist **Faith** & **Philosophy** – The **Essence** of Buddhism

For those who practice Buddhism and consider themselves 'Buddhist', their faith in the Teachings of Buddha Shakyamuni is their spiritual life; the root of all Dharma realizations – to have faith in the teachings of the Great Gautama leads to religious practice of said teachings. The indefinite practice of Dharma liberates us form all pain and suffering in this life and the next.

The attainment of enlightenment is the ultimate goal of the Buddhist – the liberation from suffering and pain until we reach true peace with ourselves as individual beings. For the individual Buddhist, the attainment of this feat relies solely on the dedication to their own Dharma practice and thus the deeper the faith in the Great Buddha, the greater their ability to satisfy their goal. It is on this basis that the philosophy of the Buddhist is born. Ultimately, the deeper one's faith in Buddhist teachings, the greater the result and the closer one comes to permanent liberation.

Now, this permanent liberation from pain and suffering cannot be confused with temporary liberation – they are by no means synonymous. We all experience temporary liberation, whether we are human beings, animals, or other matters of life. But this liberation is never permanent — it will always return in this life or in the countless lives of the future. Remember, the goal of Buddhism is liberation through the ages and through countless lifetimes – true permanence.

Samsara is the impure cycle of pain and suffering where no one ever has permanent liberation; everyone will continuously experience some form of physical or mental suffering in their lives and their future lives. This cycle of impurity has 6 realms in which we can be reborn. The lowest realm is the hell realm. This is the most impure realm of them all where the suffering of the Hell being is the utmost worst, unbearable pain. The next ascending realm is the ghost and then the animal realm. These are less impure, but suffering remains. Of the higher realms, there is the human, the demi-god and the god. It is though our acceptance of this hierarchy of life that we come to realize that any mere temporary relief from suffering in our current life is meaningless in reaching our goals; we need to attain permanent liberation from suffering in this life and all future lives that we shall live.

To the Buddhist, this can only be accomplished by placing the greatest of faith in The Great Gautama and his precious teachings. These are the only teachings in which we are taught to abandon our own self-indulgent desires and ignorant features, the source of all suffering in living beings. In the accomplishment of this abandonment, a Buddhist can eradicate the source of his own suffering and experience 'Nirvana' – absolute peace of mind. Nirvana is the Realization by Buddha himself. It is the Buddha's blind compassion to all living beings which revealed to us the goal of human life.

Nirvana can only be achieved through the blessings bestowed upon us by Buddha. Buddha bestows peace to all living being who, by themselves, would otherwise be unable to reach this state. Mental peace is the key to happiness in all living beings, says the teachings of Buddha. But given that such peace can only be attainable through the blessings of the Buddha himself, it is Buddha who is the key to true happiness. As Buddhists, this rule is practised continuously and relentlessly. It is this understanding, contemplation and practice which allows the Buddhist faith to be the only beings who have yet obtained peace and happiness in this life.

The Four **Noble** Truths

The Great Gotama recognised 4 truths to life itself – Dukkha, Samudaya, Nirodha, and Magga. These are the 4 truths that are relative to all living beings as individuals. It is these 4 truths that Buddha used to identify the suffering of life, and these truths allowed him to devise a method of spiritual liberation from such suffering.

Dukkha: The Truth of **Suffering**

Dukkha is the truth of suffering, that is, that all life is suffering. As individuals, we can likely imagine common suffering such as aging, illness and death, but in reality, suffering exists far beyond these limited concepts. On a broader scope, suffering exists in all aspects of life and life itself is then to be considered suffering – the very nature of life is the suffering of living beings. In particular, our own nature as human beings is inconsistent with the idealist perception of a life without suffering. Mankind is destined to forever be unhappy in some sense, be it wanting more or endlessly trying to reach a feat which, for all intensive purposes, is unreachable.

Samudaya: The Truth of the **Origin** of Suffering

Samudaya is the origin of suffering – where is comes from and how it originates in our lives. Of course, we can all imagine and are more than likely to have experienced some form of immediate suffering in our lives i.e. bereavement, illness, disease. But suffering does not merely exist in these physical forms. Think. What is the origin of suffering? Where does it come from? Why do we suffer in life?

The Buddha recognised that the simplistic perception of suffering was insufficient to discover its origin - Buddha went beyond our own common and superficial interpretation of suffering and its causes. And this ultimate truth? Tanha (desire). A conscious trait unique to mankind and ultimately the reason for our own suffering.

Tanha, then, is the root of suffering in our world. Buddha was able to identify 3 distinct elements of Tanha, these being:

Greed and Desire

Ignorance and Delusion

Hatred and Violence

These are ultimately the elements which constitute the suffering of mankind and identify the impossibility for man to end his own suffering.

Nirodha: The Truth of **Cessation** of Suffering

Nirodha is the concept that man can put an end and extinguish his own suffering - by releasing himself from all desire and negative attachment, man can release himself from the shackles of his kin.

It is this third noble truth which is said to be able to free a man from the cycle of rebirth. Upon achieving Nirodha, man will truly achieve contentment and nothing will remain, but for spiritual enlightenment.

Magga: The Truth of the Path to the **Cessation** of Suffering

Magga is Buddha's means of reach such spiritual liberation - a means of achieving Nirodha. The Eight-fold Path.

The **Eight**-fold Path

The Eight-fold Path is the means of achieving spiritual liberation in this life. Each division of the path should be practised simultaneously with the next. There is no set order in which to perform the divisions — they are complementary to one-another and are to be used in all acts in life.

Samma Ditthi: The Right **Understanding**

In Buddhism, it is the teachings of Buddha which are considered to be 'the right understanding' and thus, Samma Ditthi refers to the internalisation of these teachings. It is the acceptance and submission to the teachings of the Great Gotama, in particular, his four noble truths which we've covered so far. The right understanding is more than merely being aware of his teachings, but the integration and implementation of these teachings in to everything you do — the philosophy of the Buddha should become yours truly.

Samma Sankappa: The Right **Intention**

Samma Sankappa — the right intention. This refers to your reasoning behind the implementation of his teachings. To be genuine. To truly internalise his teachings to become your mindset. His teachings should manifest within you as you detach yourself from the base human qualities — desire, greed, envy. The right intention illustrates your path to enlightenment and your attitude towards life itself.

Samma Vaca: The Right **Speech**

The right speech refers to the implementation of your beliefs as a Buddhist; the way in which you interact with others. The abstinence from expressing anger, malicious intention or abuse to others. To not engage in the meaningless, shallow-minded interactions common in the world — not to argue, gossip or speak down to or about others. Your speech should be honest and true. Everything you say should have the intention of enlightening the world around you, influencing the harmony and peaceful relationship we should all strive for between one-another.

Samma Kammanta: The Right **Action**

A follow on from the right speech, the right action dictates the way in which you act. Samma Kammanta is the act of peaceful and harmonious living. You are to live with peaceful ideals and express a gentle influence on those around you. Samma Kammanta refers to both passive and active practices – to be kind to others, to become a beacon of the right example, but also not to indulge in harmful acts – killing, harming, violence. To act with honest intentions is to demonstrate your path to enlightenment.

Samma Ajiva: The Right **Livelihood**

Samma Ajiva is to live with the right intention and act. It is to abstain from living by harmful means i.e. to avoid professions which cause harm to animals, to abstain from exploiting others, to abstain from trading in harmful resources (alcohol, tobacco, drugs, to name a few). The right livelihood is to live through means which help and engage others in spiritual realisations.

Samma Vayama: The Right **Effort**

Samma Vayama is to be true in the practice of Buddhism. This is the total abolishment from negativity from your mind – it should not exist, nor grow within you. Your inner self should be harmonious and at peace – it should not be influenced negatively by anything that occurs in the physical world or in your own mind. Samma Vayama is the clarity of mind and should be present, always.

Samma Sati: The Right **Mindfulness**

Mindfulness. A foreign concept for most that many never achieve. Samma Sati is the development and acquisition of an honest awareness of self – the sensations, emotions and the physical body itself. It is to understand oneself truly to enable a better understanding of one's own path to liberty; one's path to enlightenment.

Samma Samadhi: The Right **Concentration**
To achieve the right concentration is to have a strong will power to attain the elements of the eight-fold path. It is the ability to engage with oneself in a way unfamiliar to the commons. You are to strip yourself of desires and realise within the clarity of mind that you can achieve through the practice of Buddhism and the teachings of The Buddha. It is the focus on your inner-most peace constantly.

Chapter 8: Breaking Autopilot

The very first step to really embracing mindfulness is learning to break out of autopilot mode. Autopilot is the state of existence that most of us are already living in. It is sticking to a routine and mundane schedule, rarely feeling anything aside from regular bouts of stress, dissatisfaction, discomfort, and a lack of fulfillment.

What Is "Autopilot"?

Autopilot is living your day-to-day life trapped in a mundane system of routines that do not serve you or help you to feel truly alive in your daily life. It is doing everything the same, in the way that you "should" be doing them, just to get by. It looks different for many people, but for most of us, it is living in a state of permanent survival mode. Everything we do is because we "have" to, and not because we truly "want" to. We become trapped in a series of systems that do not serve us, and that does not awaken us to the many joys and wonders of the body and world that we live in.

When we are trapped on autopilot, we often feel like the only emotions we feel are negative ones. Feelings like stress, concern, worry, frustration, sadness, depression, anxiety, and other uncomfortable emotions have a tendency to surface often when we are on autopilot. This is because our mind, body, and spirit are becoming claustrophobic and bored in the mundane routines that we are living in and are begging to be let free and provided with the opportunity to really live life. Not just live in a sense of waking up every morning and going through the motions, but **really live life.** Waking up in the morning and feeling all of your senses awaken to the world around you, breathing in the fresh air, seeing the morning sunlight, experiencing the sensations of various elements of your morning routine such as the rush of water over your body, or the tingling sensation of minty toothpaste in your mouth. The things that we often miss when we are mentally trapped in survival mode.

Breaking autopilot is mandatory if you want to begin living a mindful life that will allow you to experience peaceful and positive emotions, such as joy, serenity, gratitude, and fulfillment. Breaking autopilot is the very practice of releasing the need to stick to the mundane routine of your daily life and awaken yourself to the many wonders of the world that you face on a daily basis. It is seeing your routines from a new light, changing your routines to serve your changing needs, and finding the motivation and inspiration to interact with the world around you in ways that those trapped in autopilot simply cannot.

How Does Autopilot Affect Us?

Aside from leaving us only open to the experiences of negative emotions that build up when we feel trapped or claustrophobic in our routine, autopilot affects us in many other ways, too. Living a life strapped to autopilot and without ever truly and intentionally awakening to the life that is happening around you can have many unwanted side effects that make life itself significantly less enjoyable and fulfilling.

When we are on autopilot, we lose out on precious memories. Because our minds and bodies become so used to just "going through the motions," they never actually awaken to memory-making opportunities. That is if we even actually take any on. Autopilot leads to us missing out on experiences because we are unaware of how to actually tap into those experiences, to begin with. We are so used to bypassing them that we don't even slow down to actually watch our children grow, or see how the sun dances off of the road after it rains, or experience the changes in temperatures and worldly appearances as the seasons shift. We become so absorbed in doing what we have to that life completely passes us by and we never even notice it. Things that we value so deeply seem to be gone in an instant because we never slow down to actually experience them.

Autopilot not only robs us of memories and wonderful experiences, but it robs us of self-awareness, too. Self-awareness is more than just knowing how things make you feel and how you are truly doing on a regular basis. Self-awareness is truly a key to being able to develop the life you love. It also allows you to develop a synergy between your mind, body, and spirit. This synergy is not only blissful and peaceful, but it is also necessary when it comes to considering our health and wellness. This self-awareness allows us to recognize when parts of our health and wellness are faltering, and when we need to tune in more. It allows us to step away from the constant tendency of ignoring our health and truly nourishing ourselves and everything that contributes to our ability to being able to actually experience the world around us.

When we are mindful, we are more likely to slow down when we need to, focus on healing ourselves when we are unwell, pay attention to and avoid that which makes us unwell, and attract more of what makes us healthy and happy into our lives. It is not just a matter of becoming self-aware so that you can "know" how you are feeling and how things are affecting you. It is a matter of becoming self-aware so that you can support your own wellbeing and promote your health, wellness, peace, and happiness for years to come.

How Do You Break Autopilot?

Breaking autopilot is the very first step in designing your new mindful life, and it is a relatively easy step, too. However, it does take some sheer willpower, determination, and serious strength to embark on this step.

The step is this: you have to set the intention to become mindful, make the commitment to begin your own mindfulness practice, and stand fiercely behind your commitment so that you don't fall back into your habitual autopilot ways.

It sounds easy, right? Simply make a decision, and you're on your way.

Not so fast. Remember how we discussed that mindfulness can be intimidating and sometimes difficult to embark on, especially in the beginning? This is highly true. So, before you begin tackling the many steps and techniques provided for you within this book, I need you to start with this one: becoming mindful of your own experience with mindfulness.

Mindfulness is not something that you can decide to do and that you will then master a few minutes later. When you have habitually lived in a state of autopilot for any amount of time, breaking that habit and becoming more mindful is not easy. You may find yourself automatically doing things that you are used to, and that work directly against the very act of mindfulness itself. You may simply forget to check in, to practice, or to honor anything that mindfulness brings up for you. And that is completely okay.

Especially in the beginning, but even throughout your lifetime, you are going to run into instances where mindfulness does not come easily. You are going to find that sometimes you simply forget, or you just can't find it in you to honor what you have learned about yourself through mindfulness. You may become hard on yourself. You may become frustrated. You may search for opportunities to blame other people. Know that all of this, every part of it, is completely okay and acceptable.

While you certainly don't want to commit and go about it in a half-committed way, you also do not want to hold yourself hostage for mistakes. If you realize in hindsight that you could have been more mindful or more effective with mindfulness in any given circumstance, **forgive yourself.** Begin by forgiving yourself for not having been mindful, and be sure to also forgive yourself for the very situation itself. Mistakes happen. We are only human.

Only after you have forgiven yourself can you begin to resume your role of responsibility and consciously become aware of ways that you can handle situations differently in the future. Through regular awareness, reflection, and intention, you will find that soon you are effortlessly breaking autopilot patterns that have been a part of your habitual existence in the past and replacing them with mindfulness patterns that will promote a happy and peaceful future. This is the only way that autopilot can ever truly be broken.

Chapter 9: Why And How To Control Your Emotions

Emotions can greatly influence how we feel and treat ourselves. It is a very powerful component of our nature as humans. Gaining complete control over it is one of the first things that you should work on when aiming for a high level of self-compassion.

There are many answers to the question on why we should control our emotions. Of course, you are aware of this. If you have experienced getting angry uncontrollably, then you'll be able to enumerate the number of things that you shouldn't have done while on a high state of anger. Uncontrolled emotions cloud your judgment, take away the opportunity to apply what has been learned, and in the worst case scenario, lead to violence.

The quality of relationships we build at home and at work depends on our capability to use emotions correctly. The people around you aren't going to do the adjusting in a relationship. It all starts with you. This is why it is essential to have control over your emotions than to learn and know what to do.

At this point in time, you will probably ask about how you can control emotions. There is a scientific way of dealing with it. First of all, you have to "dissect" the process of emotional change. By knowing well the parts of the process, you will gain an awareness of where you can act.

The following stages happen when there is a change of emotion:

Occurrence of an external event or stimuli. A perfect example would be finding yourself in a scenario where you need to walk home using an unfamiliar and dark road.

Your inner voice springs into action. This is referred to by psychologists as self-talk. In the case of the event that occurred as mentioned above, your inner voice could end up telling you of the possibility of a robber waiting on the road for you.

Triggering of specific emotions. You start to feel fear, anxiety and other emotions that are related to the tone of your inner voice.

Decision-making. The action you will take will depend on what you will finally decide to do. You can proceed and dispense away the negative emotions you felt or you can choose to act on it by turning away.

If you will examine the process presented above, there are two ways through which you can control your emotions. You can act on it before or after it has been triggered. Based from this observation, you can follow the tips found below when you are trying to practice and develop control of emotions:

Get a grasp of your inner voice. It is basically you who is talking. Change the tone of the voice if it is telling you to be negative. Flood your mind with positive thoughts when you are finding this inner voice taking over what you want to happen.

When an unwanted emotion has been triggered, suppress its growth. There is a

90-second rule that you can use when it comes to this. Basically, negative emotions tend to linger and grow for only 90 seconds after they have been triggered. After that, they pass out slowly. This means that you can step back and allow this negative emotion to just ooze away instead of letting it grow and show stronger manifestations.

Practice is the key to mastering emotion control. Do the tips presented above as regularly as you can and you will find it developing into a habit. This is what makes the whole thing effective.

Controlling your emotion is essential if you want to attain greater things in terms of self-compassion, confidence, and self-esteem. While it might take some time to gain complete and automatic control over your emotions, it is not an impossible thing to do.

Chapter 10: Discovering Mindfulness

The last few years, mindfulness was one of the most popular subjects among people, especially those that are suffering from depression and anxiety. Almost everyone that has heard about mindfulness had tried to practice it and make it as part of their life. However, the real meaning of mindfulness is usually is not understood properly and it is mostly confused with other meanings, techniques and terms. So before engaging in any kind of mindfulness practice it is important to understand the real meaning of the word mindfulness and the reason why it is so important for your life.

First, you might think that mindfulness is all about breathing and to focus on your sensations on your body. Well, yes, mindfulness is these two things, but also much more. So, mindfulness is to pay attention to now and here, the present moment and not to let yourself stuck in the past and to think and worry about your future. But, it is not a technique, which means it is not a type of meditation and it is not a practice that will give you results. Actually, it is a way to be connected with your mind and feelings. But, there are simple techniques that can help you to develop mindfulness.

Mindfulness won't reduce your stress, but instead it will help you keep your stress in control. Actually the stress that everyone is experiencing in our busy life doesn't have a technique or any other way to remove it. But, by being mindful you will see the world in a better way and your attitude toward people, events and the environment will be different.

It is not all about your awareness. It will teach you how to pay attention to "now and here", to focus only on the present. What you feel now, what you are thinking now and what you are experiencing in the moment. However, it is not just to be aware but also to accept your present with kindness and curiosity and never with resistance, aggression or negativity.

In another way, mindfulness is to understand yourself in a higher level. By understanding you will be less and less affected by those negative emotions that just don't want to go away, thoughts that are all saying about the problem you are facing. It is really worth it to start taking action and to start developing your mindfulness.

Benefits of Mindfulness

Before everything else, I know that almost everyone is curious why is mindfulness so good and why do you need to start developing it. You will be surprised when you will see that even the simplest things in life are part of mindfulness and can be the best thing you can have in life.

Will the 14 benefits be enough to prove to you that mindfulness is everything you are missing in life? I hope it will, because the best motivation for everyone to start something new in life is to know the outcome and to know what they will get from it, if they practice it. So let's start.

Stress reduction – In the latest research it is proven that mindfulness is not just about reducing your stress level, but also has a connection with decreasing the levels of your stress hormone, cortisol.

Understanding your true selves – It will help you to see beyond your thoughts and start to objectively analyze yourself.

Help those with arthritis – Mindfulness might not have the power to ease the pain that people with arthritis are experiencing, but it can help lower the fatigue and stress.

Productivity – The techniques that are usually practiced to develop mindfulness actually works in a way that it changes the brain activity to protect you from mental illnesses. This is because mindfulness meditation is the number one technique that is used and practicing mindfulness meditation means you are training your body and mind. So, practicing mindfulness meditation increases the neurological connections in your brain.

Processing the pain and emotions – Practicing mediation to develop mindfulness will make you feel more Zen and focused. This is because your brain is getting help from you to take a better control on the processing your pain and emotions.

Music – When you are mindful, you will hear and listen with more attention and clarity. Your focus on music will be improved and it will help you truly enjoy and also experience what you are listening to, at the moment.

The four elements – The health benefits that person gets form mindfulness can be separated into 4 elements; Self-awareness, body awareness, the regulation of attention and the regulation of emotions.

Resting from fixation – Of course, everyone needs to think at some point. The thing is that the mind knows to wander away when you are having stressful thoughts of your past and your future. You replay difficult and painful experiences that were in your past and you think about worst scenarios for the future. This will exhaust you and it won't result in productivity. Learning to pay attention to the present is a welcome relief from the stressful patterns and bad experiences of your past life and for your future expectations.

It will take you out of yourself – Have you noticed that number 1 discursive thinking is actually self-focused? It is very energizing and refreshing when you open your awareness to the environment and the world around you and not to be preoccupied with your own personal stories. Mindfulness, as you already read, won't take away the pain, but it will help you cope with the sensation and when the intensity takes over your entire sense, you think and feel nothing else but the sensation of pain.

Simple activity can be an adventure – Cleaning the table after you and your family had dinner sounds very boring. But when you are mindfully aware it can become your own adventure. To find the best way to take all the dishes at once to the kitchen; to find the right size container to store all the food that wasn't eaten; then to transfer the food without making a mess. This engagement, which is intentional, is what is happening in the moment and this generates curiosity and it won't be boring.

Free from judgment – The awareness that is non-judgmental of what presents itself to your senses is the golden key and feature of mindfulness. You will become an impartial observer and friendly person, one that is free to let go of judging. Remember, this doesn't mean that you shouldn't take action to stop and prevent harm to someone or to yourself. Mindfulness, just like Buddhist practices, it is for alleviating suffering. So, once you develop mindfulness you will know when to abandon your impartial observation and grab that person who is about to step in front of a car.

Making wise choices – When your mind is blocked with every stressful thought that piles up all the time, it is very hard to see through it. You get confused very fast and instead of becoming reflective you become reactive. Then that moment happens when you react to someone, that you regret later. By practicing mindfulness, for both unpleasant and pleasant experiences you will most likely be aware of your reactive tendencies. You will be able to catch yourself and take a breath to choose another skillful way to respond.

It will open your mind and heart – Pema Chödrön, one of the best Tibetan Buddhist teachers describes this like, "Letting the world speak for itself". Later you will learn about how to develop mindfulness and there are many ways to practice it. So, this quote can be a mindful practice outside of your meditation. You can say it wherever you are, silently to yourself and this way you will develop your mindfulness. The world will give you the answer for life experience.

Helping you to succeed – Developing and practicing mindfulness can help you improve your performance. It helps to handle negative emotions and feelings and thereby clears your thought process. When you thinking is clear you can make business decisions with a lot of confidence and clarity.

Chapter 11: Mindfulness-Based Stress Reduction

How to Not Take Our Thoughts Personally
Questioning Our Narrative
Your narrative is the story of your life. It is all the hurts, successes, failures, and accomplishments that you have accumulated over the course of your life. When you feel unworthy it feels like you are flawed and then must hide all your faults from everyone, or else you fear you may be shunned. However, concealing flaws, pretending, and withholding faults from others will make you begin to feel like an outcast, which then can make you believe that you truly are flawed. This cycle of self-doubting and self-judgments can leave you feeling like you are not complete. By practicing mindfulness and self-compassion, you can see the pains within your own narrative. This will help you to overcome the thinking that your

negative story defines who you are. It is not who you are.

The stories we tell, predominantly the ones do not know are in the back of our psyche, can strongly form who we are, and from there the choices that we make. Becoming acquainted with our inner stories and how they influence how we communicate with others is a characteristic of becoming self-aware, and a large foundation of mindfulness. But it can be complicated to separate ourselves from the stories that make up our being unless we are aware of them, and from there try to understand where they began. Each one of us can be a storyteller, it is a natural way of organizing your worlds. Through this process, the brain can categorize those memories as a way to use in the future to help calculate events, relationships, and experiences. Four millennia all cultures have used stories as a way to explain everything for how they hunted to wisdom, and pass on their traditions

The next opportunity you get when you are stopped at traffic or waiting in line at the supermarket, consider what your mind is doing. You may be surprised to find yourself recounting a story. It may be plans for the weekend, a recent article you read, or recounting a conversation you had recently that did not end well. No matter what it is, this is a story, all adding to your life's overall narrative.

How do your stories begin? It all starts at an early age. As young children, we all test the world around us in an attempt to learn what things are, and what the outcomes will be. They even tend to have exaggerated long narratives when they play because they are trying to see what fits and what does not. As an adult, you do the same thing. How it differs is that it is all in your head, which then determines our behavior and how we react to situations.

Most of the basic narratives that are created about your identity are shaped by how you were raised, what your parents perceived, and your significant others. As you receive consistent feedback, the more those stories take hold within you. As you get older, you tend to seek out relationships and experiences that reinforce that narrative. This is called confirmation bias. These biases tend to influence how you view yourself and who you become tremendously.

Take for example the story of a young child whose older sibling has been dubbed the genius. Imagine how that younger sibling may feel knowing he may never be as smart as his older brother. He enters school, and starts to learn, and struggles because he knows he is not as smart as his brother. However, as he ages, he soon realized that he has a natural ability in something, like math or English. He reaches high school and can take advanced courses. Through this, he has effectively managed to rewrite his narrative that he had been preconditioned to. However, despite that amazing story of overcoming his predetermines vision of himself, when presented with a stressful situation, that original insecurity of not feeling smart enough may arise, causing you to feel even more overwhelmed or anxious.

Why does any of this matter? Because over years of accumulating these narratives, they have shaped you in some positive and some negative ways, wiring your brain so to speak to react and function a certain way, causing you to be inflexible when it comes to mental or emotional events. We tend to remember the negative and painful stories better than the positives. This is called negativity bias. Even though your narrative may influence your perception or reactions, it does not mean you are trapped to live them out. By paying attention to your mental awareness, you will be able to start breaking down your personal awareness, and when you are stressed, this can be an invaluable tool. That inner voice tends to get louder when you are stressed, overworked, and tired. So, by learning to pay attention to that inner voice, you can slowly start to rewire your brain.

This is one of the main goals of mindfulness. Learning to observe and pay attention to your body non-judgmentally. This takes practice, and you need to learn how to find those stories first. Here is a simple exercise for you to try as a way to identify your narrative.

Start by writing down what you feel your identity is. Simple phrases like "I am strong," or "I like to help others," or "I am really good at my job." You may also want to include things like how you were raised, experiences, family beliefs, or any other examples that shaped how you view yourself now.

Now that you have written all that down, take each one and ask yourself these questions regarding that specific phrase or experience:

Can I change this story or am I deciding to live it?

Does this story still apply to me?

Whose story is this? Mine or somebody else's?

How did this story originate?

Am I unhappy because of this story

Being aware of your personal narrative contributes to mindfulness because you are learning what some of your inner thoughts are, that mindless chatter that is always there. By learning what causes it, you can practice mindfulness and learn to readjust your thinking, even your story, as well as reduce some of that needless stress that can arise when those negative stories come up.

Mindfulness and Being Non-Judgmental

Before you can practice non-judgment in mindfulness, it is a good idea to understand what non-judgment means. By now you should begin to understand what mindfulness means, it is the ability to be aware. Awareness on its own does not have judgment. Judgment is a thought process that can come through the awareness. This is not the kind of judgment that produces prejudices or judging someone to be inferior to you. It is the judgment of making decisions, taking making choices and putting them in the proper place. Example: When you feel that stress or depression is starting to affect you, it is important to be aware of the signs of them, then make the judgment to begin helping yourself in some way.

Non-judgment in mindfulness is used if the brain is left to its own devices, it will judge things automatically as right or wrong, fair or unfair, good or bad, important or unimportant, etc. The brain does this so fast that experiences are automatically processed as one or the other before you can take stock of it all. Mindfulness stops all this, and focuses on being aware of when these judgments are taking place, and then using that to take a brand new viewpoint.

The hard part of all of this is learning to be aware of when your brain has started to automatically judge something or a situation. If we are aware, we can take a pause and reflect on it. By doing this you will be able to take that new point of view, and then enter the non-judgmental decision-making process which mindfulness teaches.

Mindfulness and Greed

Greed is an innate feeling we all experience. The mind always is looking for something more. This can range anywhere from doing something new to gaining something that may bring pleasure. However, these moments of happiness last only a moment, and then what happens? We start to want more, possibly the same things or something else.

Greed is considered to be one of three unwholesome states of mind which are aversion, delusion, and greed. The defilements of the mind are a common teaching in meditation. If you have greedy thoughts, it will help them to grow, and this will start a cycle of never-ending actions which can eventually cause pain to others and yourself. Ending this cycle can be extremely hard because we live in a society that likes us to look to outside sources for happiness.

So how do we overcome wants and desires which feed into the natural tendency of the mind to be greedy? Here is an exercise you can try that will help you refocus your mind away from those desires.

Imagine something that you want, really, really, want. Imagine yourself having that item. How does it feel to have it?

Now let it go. Taking a deep breath, and using mindfulness, see the object for what it is, but without needing to be possessed.

Think of what you already have. Appreciate it. How does it feel?

Now that you have let go of the object to be obtained, how do you feel knowing that you have enough right now?

Greed is encouraged in our world because we have been conditioned to believe that more is always better. By practicing mindfulness, you can train yourself to have these thoughts, and be content with what you have right now.

How to simplify your thoughts and desires

What is the best possible amount: Find the middle ground. By trial and error, you will discover what your optimal amount is, or what satisfies you.

Wants versus needs: Society bombards us daily with things we need to buy, consume, and accumulate, and this all feeds into our greed. The simplest way to not fall for marketing scams is to take stock of what you have and ask yourself "Do I NEED this, or do I WANT this." Only then will you be able to stop the greed cycle.

Avoid the trap of self-fulfilling prophecies.

What exactly is a self-fulfilling prophecy? To be able to practice this in mindfulness, you must know what this means. Basically, a self-fulfilling prophecy is when any positive or negative expectation of a circumstance, event or a person, that can affect your behavior which will cause you to act in a way that makes those expectations come true. A good example of this would be when you first meet someone, if you have a negative expectation of that person that you will not like something about them or the person as a whole, when you meet this person you will act in such a way that will cause the other person to do exactly what you thought, something to make you dislike them.

This cycle of almost self-destruction can wreak havoc when it comes to people with social anxieties, low self-esteem, and when it comes to career advancement. This self-fulfillment will eventually do exactly as you fear because your behaviors based on your negative or fearful thoughts, will show through to others and then they reciprocate those same manners.

So how can you stop this horrible trap? Mindfulness. Practicing a simple self-affirmation exercise daily can help you to overcome your tendencies to set yourself up for failure.

Mindfulness and feeling Joy for Others

A lot of people are scared to show genuine empathy for others because it means they may open themselves up to the possibility of becoming everyone else's pain and suffering. Empathy can be viewed as a stressor because dealing with everyone else's problems can cause exhaustion, and burn out.

However, in mindfulness, you can instead increase your ability to feel other people's

joys, instead of building a wall against their stress. There can be great benefits to this, and it is called positive empathy, instead of the empathy that eventually causes you to want to hide from people.
Studies have shown that when you have empathy for other people's pain, your brain will emulate pain of its own. The same is true of positive empathy, and when you have happiness over someone else's happiness, the brain will resonate with this as well. When you have these positive experiences, it has been shown to give more satisfaction, happiness, and peace of mind. It can also help you to gain support, greater trust, and satisfaction in close relationships.

Positive empathy, or feeling joy for others, does more than make you feel good, it can also help you to want to help others to thrive, and thus you have a stronger will to act on those feelings. Noticing joy can be easier than you think. When you think of joy, it usually presents itself as that giant smile, delight, cheers, and hugs. However, joy can be a lot smaller than that and can be found all around you. You can find joy in a delicious meal, a favorite song that comes on the radio, and the joy of hearing laughter. And these are just a few of the possible smaller joys you can find everywhere. As you practice mindfulness and awareness, the opportunities to see the joy in ordinary moments will gradually increase.

Mindfulness and liberation from suffering

Suffering and happiness cannot exist without each other. You cannot learn to be compassionate if you have never experienced suffering. However, suffering can become toxic when it is not cared for properly. You harden your heart and become overwhelmed. This then makes it impossible for you to experience compassion.

Mindfulness holds that pain is not the enemy, nor does it want to get rid of that pain. It seeks instead to help you better understand yourself and why you are in pain. By practicing mindfulness, you can start to understand what your causes of pain and suffering are, and then you will be able to liberate yourself from them.

Compassion can only arise when you mindfully take a look at your suffering and respond to it with care. As you practice mindfulness more and more, you will soon begin to discover which gestures of kindness and joy will help to open up your heart. Everyone is different in what appeals to their compassion. Once you have identified some triggers that help you, you will soon learn that even the smallest gesture of compassion will open you up to greater happiness and help to curb your suffering.

Chapter 12: Mindful Breathing Meditation

Of all the different mindfulness practices in the world, there is nothing more basic yet profound as mindful breathing. Your breath is the essence of your life and without it, your consciousness will cease to exist. Therefore, it would be wise to begin all your meditation sessions with this foundational practice.

Mindful breathing meditation is the simple practice of becoming fully aware of your own breath. Contrary to what some believe, you do not try to alter your breath during this meditation, such as by making each breath deeper or longer. Instead, you are simply noticing each natural breath as it comes and goes.

How to do Mindful Breathing Meditation

You can practice mindful breathing whether you are sitting, standing or lying down. The standard meditation session itself can last for as little as a minute or for as long as 20 minutes. It really is up to you, but if you have always struggled to stay still, then you can surely spare 1 or 2 minutes to practice mindful breathing.

Here are the steps to do it:

Step 1: Get to a comfortable posture. You can sit on a cushion on the floor, on a chair, or lie down on a mattress. Ensure that the back is straight with the shoulders relaxed. Set your timer.

Step 2: Relax your eyelids. They may droop or close. Adopt the attitude of openness and curiosity towards the present moment. You can say, "I am open, curious and meditating."

Step 3: Draw your full attention towards your breath. Do not change your breathing pattern, but if you cannot help but do so, avoid criticizing yourself for it is perfectly fine.

Notice how your body breathes in the air through the nostrils, down the windpipe and into the lungs.

Become aware of how your ribcage and abdominal muscles expand as your lungs are filled with air.

Notice how your lungs push up the air through your windpipe and out of your nostrils.

Step 4: Continue to focus on these sensations of breathing. When you hear the timer, allow yourself a minute or two to come out of the meditative state gently. There is no need to rush.

Whenever your mind wanders to other thoughts and sensations, simply acknowledge this change of path, but avoid following it.

Do not criticize the thoughts as it is perfectly natural for them to be there. All you have to do is imagine yourself as a mountain and the thoughts as passing clouds. They are there, but you remain stable and strong.

Once the thoughts and sensations pass you by, draw your focus back towards your breathing in a soft and gentle way.

After reading these steps, you should try breathing meditation this very moment. Spare even just one minute of your time right now to practice it. Remember that there is no right or wrong to do it. What matters is that you do it.

After trying the breathing meditation, come back to this page to move on.

So, what do you think of breathing meditation? It is not as intimidating as what some may believe it to be, after all! In fact, it is so simple.

If you had noticed that your thoughts wandered off several times, do not worry because your mind simply has not adjusted yet to the idea of focusing on the core of the present moment, your breath. Just simply come back to noticing your breath, when the mind strays again simply come back to the breath again.

Through practice, you can condition your mind to become accustomed to the stillness, making yourself ready for longer and more in-depth meditation later on. In the next chapter, you will learn the next foundational type of mindfulness meditation, which is sitting meditation.

Chapter 13: Understanding Stress

When we feel upset, angry, disappointed or hurt, we experience a feeling of physical or emotional strain or pressure— a feeling of real or perceived disruption of our state of balance. We call this feeling "stress".

Stress is our response to the environmental stimuli and stressors, which can impact our very way of existing. When stress occurs, we experience a sense of disharmony and a lack of balance within ourselves. According to psychologist Richard S Lazarus, stress occurs when an individual perceives that their demands exceed the personal and social resources they are able to mobilize. Lazarus's theory is the most commonly accepted definition of stress.

Stress is a universal experience and we all feel stressed from time to time— it's a natural part of being human. Stress is not always bad. The way we perceive stress determines how great an impact the stress will have on us. The stress of a creative and exhilarating work benefits us, while the stress of failure and humiliation can wreak havoc in our lives.

The feeling of stress is not pleasant. During the moments of stress, we try to regain our physical and mental balance. And when the balance is regained, we not only feel relieved but also feel confident about our ability to handle stress in the future. Failure to regain the balance makes the stress stronger, which makes us feel exhausted and sick.

Stress and Our Body

You might have heard the term "Fight or Flight" response, the body's vital warning system that is activated when we are confronted with an object of fear. It is also called "Hyperarousal". When we feel panicked, our animal body tells us to fight the threat, or run away from it. This mechanism was evolved to protect us by reacting quickly to life-threatening situations. The fight or flight response increases our internal awareness of danger and transforms all the body's resources to a heightened state of readiness.

During this process, our system goes through a near-instantaneous sequence of hormonal secretions, especially epinephrine and norepinephrine, which causes several psychological changes including an increase in heart rate and blood pressure. The blood glucose level goes high, pupils dilate and muscles in several areas of the body get stiff and tense for increased speed and strength. The digestive and immune system slow down or stop to allow more energy for emergency functions. These changes are intended to help humans and other mammals to survive a physical threat by preparing them to fight the threat off or flee to safety.

However, this mechanism is essentially the body's reaction to a perceived attack. The perceived threat can be unreal, but it will still activate this response. To further understand the nature of this response, we can use the analogy of a smoke detector. The smoke alarm goes off when there is the danger of fire. But as it can't distinguish between the smoke from burning bacon and a house fire, it can go off even when there's no danger present. Likewise, the human body also can't distinguish between a real and perceived threat— it only responds to inputs it receives from the brain. That's the reason why even the ordinary stressors we face on a daily basis, like college exams or work deadlines, can trigger the fight and flight response.

Once the perceived threat is gone, our system is supposed to return to normal. However, in the case of chronic stress, the body remains in a more or less constant state of alertness. This gives rise to other symptoms and contributes to other long-term problems.

The Three Types of Stress

Not everyone experience stress the same way. Different people may experience different physical and emotional symptoms of stress and respond differently. Also, the perception of a stressor can be different for different people. For instance, one may find public speaking very stressful, while others may enjoy it. Stress can be short-term or long-lasting. Based on the duration and frequency, the psychologist classified stress into three types:

Acute stress

Episodic stress

Chronic stress

Acute Stress: This is a very common and the most known form of stress. Our anticipation of near future, or the memories of the recent past generates this stress. Acute stress can quickly escalate. It appears suddenly and feels quite intense when it surfaces, but it also disappears quickly. As soon as the situation is resolved, the stress subsides. Acute stress typically occurs during life's crisis— this might be an accident, sudden bereavement or other traumatic events. However, ordinary stressors like interviews and work deadlines can also trigger acute stress.

Acute stress experience is not always unpleasant. Sometimes it can bring excitement and thrill to our lives. For instance, activities like roller coaster rides and bungee jumping may bring about acute stress, yet brings excitement and joy.

However, even these enjoyable events can turn uncomfortably stressful if they last longer. If the stress produced from these activities is more than we can handle, we may experience symptoms like dizziness, vomiting, and shortness of breath. As acute stress is a temporary condition, it typically does not last long enough to cause damage to our health.

Episodic acute stress: People, who struggle to cope with many simultaneous demands of their time and attention, may experience frequent episodes of acute stress. When acute stress happens frequently, it is called episodic acute stress. This kind of repetitive stress episode may occur when someone is confronted with a series of very real stressful challenges. Sufferers of episodic acute stress seem to go through many different disastrous situations and live in chaos and disorganization. They take on too much and fail to cope with self-imposed demands and pressures claiming their attention.

Chronic stress: Some stresses are ongoing. When stress is experienced for a prolonged period of time, it is called chronic stress. This type of stress occurs when there is a persistent worry and the sufferer never sees an escape from the stressors and stops seeking solutions. Situations such as war and conflict, dysfunctional home, relentless job demands, financial struggle, family abuse, which takes months even years to resolve, can trigger chronic stress condition.

There are two types of chronic stress— Clinical chronic stress and sub-clinical chronic stress. If the cause of the chronic stress is recognizable, then it is called clinical chronic stress. If the source of stress occurs within the body (i.e. adrenal syndrome, food intolerance, electromagnetic radiation) and generally remains obscured from senses— it is called subclinical chronic stress.

Negative Effects of Stress

Although we rarely need to be in fight-or-flight mode, some degree of stress is required to function properly. However, when the stress level remains longer than necessary, it wreaks havoc on our health. Toxic stress may harm your body even though you might not realize it. Chronic stress negatively affects almost every system of our body.

According to the American Medical Association, stress is the basic cause of more than 60% of human diseases and illnesses.

Persistent stress can augment the risk of long-term health problems like diabetes and hypertension. Stress can be also blamed for accident and injury in the workplace.

Chronic stress often leads to addictions to drugs and alcohol.

Although rare, negative acute stress can cause serious health damage. In rare cases, sudden emotional stress can lead to heart attacks and strokes.

The morbidity and mortality associated with stress-related diseases are rapidly increasing worldwide. Too much stress can increase suicidal thoughts in high risk individuals. Stress pushes most suicide victims over the edge and forces them to take their own lives.

Common Signs and Symptoms

Most of us are so used to being stressed, we think that it's normal until it builds up gradually and becomes a serious problem. Stress signs can sometimes be too subtle to be identified as problematic. Some stress symptoms can be mistaken for other health problems. Therefore it is important to identify the signs of stress overload. Here are some common symptoms:

Cognitive/emotional symptoms
Restlessness and agitation

Depression and general unhappiness
Difficulty to focus
Confusion
Difficulty thinking in a logical sequence
Poor memory
Racing thoughts
Anger or irritation
Mood swings
Lack of judgment
A feeling of loneliness or worthlessness
Compulsive behavior
Feeling overwhelmed
Little interest in appearance, punctuality
Increased frustration
Apathy
Other mental and emotional health problems
Physical symptoms
Lightheadedness, dizziness, faintness
Pounding or racing heart, chest pain
Cold or sweaty hands, feet
Tense muscles, aches, and pains
Tremors, trembling of lips, hands
Butterflies in stomach
Dry mouth and difficulty swallowing
Indigestion, irritable bowel, constipation

Dry mouth, problems swallowing
Sleep problems, insomnia
Hair loss
Sweating when not physically active
Sweaty palms
Change in sex drive
Nausea
Headaches
Chest pain
Frequent colds and infection
Low energy
Ulcers, gastritis
Hypertension, heart disease
Pains in shoulders neck and low back, sore jaw
Clenched jaw and grinding teeth
Severe cramps, missed periods (women)
Erectile dysfunction, premature ejaculation (men)
Unexplained rashes or skin irritations
Weight gain around the waistline.

Behavioral Symptoms

Change in appetite— eating too much or too little
Procrastinating and avoiding responsibilities

Sleeping too little or too much
Social withdrawal
Increased use of alcohol, drugs or cigarettes
Risk-taking behavior
Suicidal talk or behavior
Exhibiting nervous behaviors, such as nail biting and fidgeting
Lack of punctuality and absenteeism
Relationship conflicts
Fast/abrupt speech
Unhealthy eating habits

Reducing Stress With Mindfulness

Our state of mind plays a vital role in determining our experience of stress symptoms. The symptoms we experience during the moments of stress aren't usually under our conscious control. But we can use indirect methods to influence them. Mindfulness is one of those indirect methods we can use to change our perception of the stress symptoms. By changing our perception, we can dramatically reduce our stress. Mounting evidence from hundreds of studies strongly indicates that practicing mindfulness helps people experience a calmer life and enables them to better handle stressful and demanding situations. Practicing mindfulness gradually develops inner strength, so that the future stressors have less impact on our emotional well-being. Mindfulness is increasingly becoming popular as a stress-relief strategy that actually works. In the upcoming chapters, we will learn how to effectively use mindfulness as a tool for the reduction of stress, improving health and the quality of life.

Chapter 14: Exploring The Techniques

And Principles Of Meditation

Before examining the many techniques of meditation, it may be helpful to first understand, and then explore several different kinds of meditation. Obviously, there are many, including Transcendental, Hindu, Taoist, Zen, Buddhist, and Mindfulness Meditation, among others. Practiced by people from all walks of life, each has essentially the same objective: to quiet our busy lives and overcome years of habitual conditioning of the mind with quiet thought and reflection.

First we'll explore three popular types of meditation techniques that a beginner can master with a lot of dedication, and a little time. Then we'll look at some of the earliest forms of meditation to see how the various techniques engage the mind in different ways to produce different outcomes. To say they are all equal or generate the same responses is a myth.

Though most provide relaxation, and all involve some form of breathing techniques, "research has shown that not all produce the same physiological, psychological or behavioral effects". 4

SITTING MEDITATION

One of the most popular and recognized forms of meditation is Sitting Meditation. The 1st Century Lexicon Dictionary describes sitting meditation as: "A session of meditation undertaken while seated, aimed toward calming the mind and reaching insight as to the nature of the mind." 5 There are also references elsewhere that refer to sitting meditation as zazen, from Zen Buddhism. Zazen can quite possibly be described as "returning home to care for one's self". On the surface, sitting meditation (or any form of meditation, for that matter) may seem foreign and complicated, but it's not. Still, some people are frustrated by sitting still and trying to concentrate without distraction. Sitting Meditation does take practice and dedication to work, so perseverance is key.

To begin, find a quiet place and time to sit comfortably. Believe it or not, this can be on a bus, in the passenger seat of a car, in an airplane, or wherever you have 15-20 minutes of quiet time. However, if you are easily distracted, and this may be a problem initially, then sitting in a quiet place where you will be undisturbed is best.

Sit upright, but not rigid, with both feet on the ground — and do not cross you legs. Close your eyes and picture your surroundings, while paying close attention to whatever is on your mind at the moment. As you sit, try to relax. Slow your breathing, like the waves of the ocean. Commonly, within a few minutes, thoughts or memories may surface. Sitting meditation doesn't always promise "happy thoughts". Sometimes, thoughts and feelings may be painful, and not easily dismissed. Understand that whatever thoughts you may have — joy, delight, or anger, pain, and irritation — it's important to recognize the thoughts are real, think on them, then slowly let them go. No need to pretend they don't exist, but try to focus and accept each thought. But be aware of negative thoughts, and don't let them consume you. This may be a simple idea, but it can be hard to implement. Remember, sitting meditation is meant to calm you from mental and emotional stress. It's not meant to erase your nagging problems, but to help you better deal with whatever issues are troubling you at the moment.

WALKING MEDITATION

Walking Meditation is meditation in action. Simply put, the act of walking is the main focus. There are two obvious differences between sitting and walking meditation: during walking meditation, our eyes are open and we are concentrating on our walking, not on sitting. The natural rhythm of alternating your steps and swinging your arms helps the mind, and yes, even the body, relax. Take slow, deep breaths. If your mind begins to wander, or your thoughts begin to take you to another place, or you get distracted by another person or the bark of a dog, or you begin to tense up, return your focus to the natural tempo of walking.

There is no wrong or right place to walk, although out-of-doors, enjoying the sunshine, singing birds, or even a rain shower, can better help you relax into a state of meditation than walking in a mall or other public place where you can be easily distracted. This may seem impossible at first, as so many distractions can appear out of nowhere, but when you find yourself concentrating on something other than putting one foot in front of the other, return your focus once again to that natural tempo. You'll get it.

If possible, it's best if you can set aside 15-20 minutes of free time, instead of trying to meditate while running to class, or speed-walking for exercise. Give walking your undivided attention and the rewards of walking meditation will become crystal clear.

"When you look at the sun during your walking meditation, the mindfulness of the body helps you to see that the sun is in you; without the sun there is no life at all and suddenly you get in touch with the sun in a different way." **— Thich Nhat Hanh** [6]

MINDFULNESS MEDITATION

There can't be enough said about the many benefits and rewards of mindfulness meditation. Mindfulness meditation is one of the most popular forms of meditation, as it can be integrated into most any daily activity, from drinking a cup of tea, to showering; during yoga, and even when mowing the lawn.

Imagine having control over your mind, instead of the other way around. Mindfulness meditation is also one of the most helpful forms of meditation as it helps train our minds and bodies to remain calm and relaxed while meditating on the things in life that we can not always change. Even more importantly, it is also about being mindful and aware of the things in our lives that we do have a certain amount of control over. For instance: Let's say you are plagued with anxiety and hesitate going into a gym and exercising in front of a crowd, but decide to go anyway. Once there, instead of concentrating on what others are doing, try to focus your attention on simply walking on the treadmill, or bicycling on a stationary bike; remind yourself why you need to exercise and what great benefits can be attained — thoughts you have control over.

Mindfulness meditation helps us to understand, and therefore accept who we are, just as we are. It gives us the tools to stop beating up on ourselves, or be swallowed up by the anxiety and pain so often experienced in life. Mindfulness meditation is unique in that it doesn't teach us to be different from who we already are, but helps us be aware and present in whatever is happening in our lives, not matter what that is. So, instead of trying to get away from difficult circumstances, mindfulness meditation helps us practice being in them. Equally, we can achieve the same with pleasant experiences. Surprisingly, we sometimes have even more trouble dealing with pleasant thoughts and experiences because we are afraid these "happy times" won't last or will fade away too soon. Mindfulness meditation helps us face each experience, good or bad, head-on.

To better understand how to implement mindfulness meditation as part of your daily routine, let's break it down into a few easy steps to get started.

First: Set aside a few minutes during your day. It helps if this is the same time every day, as it will help you stick to a routine. This may be difficult to do initially as the responsibilities in our lives can make it challenging to set aside even a few minutes. However, we all need time for ourselves, so become protective of 5-15 minutes of well-deserved time alone.

Second: Get comfortable. Obviously, it's more difficult to "get comfortable" when exercising or walking, but getting comfortable is more about relaxing than sitting or wearing loses-fitting clothing. Relax. That's the key. The floor works well for many people, whereas others are much more comfortable sitting on a chair, with feet on the floor — cross-legged.

Third: Set a timer. Use your phone, stopwatch, or even a kitchen timer. Whichever works best. If you're just beginning, start with 5-10 minutes, and work your way up to 15-20 minutes as you fall into your routine. Don't get discouraged if it takes a while to progress, and don't give up. Remember, practice makes perfect. Or, as someone once said, a journey begins with one step.

Fourth: Take slow, deep breaths. Deep breathing helps settle your nerves. There is a practice designed by Dr. Andrew Weil, an American medical doctor, teacher, and best-selling author on holistic health, that suggests breathing deep into your diaphragm through your nose for a count of four, holding your breath for a count of seven, and breathing out through your mouth for a count of eight. It works. Breathing techniques, such as this are vital for all meditation practices.

Fifth: Remember, if you lose focus on your breathing, or if you realize your attention has wandered, return your focus to your breathing, while doing your best to let go of any distracting thoughts or feelings. Always return your attention to your breathing. It is relaxing and comforting. It will help you unwind and loosen up from everyday worry and stress.

Sixth: Keep your eyes closed when the timer goes off. When you're ready, open your eyes. Acknowledge your success and be thankful for the time you set aside in your day.

Of course, there are countless other forms of meditation. Most fall into three or four general categories, or a combination thereof. Many researchers classify meditation techniques into only two categories: non-concentrative and concentrative. Either way, there may be an overlap with these techniques or one meditation technique can be both concentrative and non-concentrative. The following are a few of the most common and popular practices of meditation.

Understanding each type of meditation is challenging because of the difficulty in grasping a clear and concise definition of each practice. There are dozens of resources that will assign different names to each, or try to squeeze them into only one form of meditation. Understanding the basics, however, will allow you to research further into what meditation practice works best, and is best for your needs.

FOCUSED OR CONCENTRATION MEDITATION

One of the earliest and considered least difficult practices of meditation is known as Focused or Concentration Meditation, which has its roots in Zen Meditation, Om, Shine or Samadhi, and Chakra meditation.

While non-concentrative meditation can be frustrating for some people as it requires focusing on the present moment, the purpose of focused or concentration meditation is building concentration. It involves intently focusing on almost anything involving the senses, such as a sound, an object, smells, or simply breathing, and then staying in the present moment with your concentration on that one sense.

As in most forms of meditation, it takes concentration in order to focus on an object, breathing techniques, the tempo of walking, music, a sound, or a picture. Getting rid of distractions allows sustained focus, and helps you to remain calm and relaxed.

On a side note, Transcendental Meditation, or TM, is sometimes considered a focused meditation, and sometimes, not. It depends on the source. Because it is mantra-based, and therefore requires "concentration" on a mantra, this technique, for all intents and purposes, meets the definition of a concentration meditation. However, many TM organizations claim "focused attention" is not the aim of TM, but instead it is meant to simply take us to a state of enlightenment so we experience an inner calm and quiet state, even when busy. Because of these contrasting viewpoints, Transcendental Meditation often falls into a practice all its own.

SELF-TRANSCENDING MEDITATION

Transcendental Meditation, or TM, is probably one of the most well-known meditation practices. In fact, many well-known television and movie personalities use it: Ellen DeGeneres, Jerry Seinfeld and Hugh Jackson (just to name a few), swear by its benefits. Rising to popularity in the early 1960s, "TM requires very little mental effort or relaxation techniques, and consists of silently repeating a mantra; any of those parts of the Vedic literature which consist of the metrical psalms of praise, or any sacred word or syllable used as an object of concentration and embodying some aspect of spiritual power". 7

The Cleveland Clinic's definition of Transcendental Meditation is: "Transcendental Meditation does not focus on breathing or vocalized chanting, like other forms of meditation. Instead, it encourages a restful state of mind beyond thinking... A 2009 study found Transcendental Meditation helped alleviate stress in college students, while another found it helped reduce blood pressure, anxiety, depression and anger." 8

Although TM is considered a mental technique, it has been shown to also have extensive physiological benefits as well, as it allows the mind to deeply concentrate inwardly. In fact, a Stanford University study found that: "TM was twice as effective as any other meditation practice at relieving stress and anxiety. This study was a meta-analysis of 146 independent studies, and was published in the Journal of Clinical Psychology. It is said to automatically lead to the experience of "consciousness itself", the screen of awareness without any objects of awareness, a low-stress state called transcendental or pure consciousness". 9

REFLECTIVE MEDITATION

"Reflective meditation is also known as analytical meditation and refers to disciplined thinking". 10 Sometimes called mindful reflection, this practice helps us become closer to ourselves via our emotions, our thoughts, and our body, often referred to as balance. This practice also allows us become aware of "the now," and how we are feeling at a particular moment, while recognizing we are living in this present moment and time. Reflective meditation includes walking meditation, Yoga, Tai Chi, and can even include music and art.

Reflective meditation practice is a bit like disciplined thinking, such as concentrating on just one question, one problem, or one thought. If our mind wanders from that one thing, we return to it. Traditional forms of reflective meditation teach us to gain insight into relationships, a philosophy or scripture, or even the meaning of life and death in order to find a solution and reach a better understanding of ourselves.

Reflective meditation and yoga go hand-in-hand, and are practiced to help us become stress-free. Many people practice yoga as a form of exercise. Yet as a technique of meditation, yoga offers much more than that. Yoga aims to connect the body and mind through thoughtful breathing and movement. It helps relieve stress and anxiety, and there is some evidence that yoga can help manage high blood pressure and ease chronic pain as well.

GUIDED MEDITATION

This form of meditation is guided; or in other words, a teacher is present, or an audio recording or video is used to walk you through meditation, one step at a time. While in a state of deep relaxation, your mind is open to positive suggestions from a teacher or audio/video designed to improve your life; be that spiritual development, emotional healing or elimination of anxiety.

Guided meditation practice has been referred to as "intense" by some followers, as it focuses on deep physical relaxation and healing at an almost celestial or spiritual level. That being said, it is also one of the most enjoyable ways to reduce stress and bring about positive mental and physical healing. Guided meditation can be as short as a few minutes, or as long as an hour, depending on a person's needs.

After examining just a few of the many meditation techniques, what kind of meditation is best for you? The answer may be all of the above. But the general tendency is to start with the same basic principles and techniques found in all forms of meditation. Commit to the long haul. Even with the best of intensions, practicing meditation on a regular basis can be easier said than done. Some people consider meditation "hard work", and we all know it's easy to put off what may seem difficult to master. Stick with it. With a little commitment on your part, you will soon come to understand the many benefits.

In a nutshell: Find a quiet place either inside or outside to relax, and make sure you won't be disturbed. Be aware of your breathing, and remember that although your mind may wander, let the thoughts linger for a moment, then return to calm, relaxed breaths. Don't stress. This might be most important for beginners. If you can't sit still, or if your breathing is erratic, or something outside catches your attention and you can't let it go, don't beat yourself up. As mentioned previously, practice makes perfect — you'll catch on.

Chapter 15: Adopting Mindfulness As A Way Of Life

As you will discover, mindfulness is not only seated meditation during which you focus on your breath for x number of minutes. No, it's so much more. When you adopt mindfulness in your daily life, you can begin to see the benefits pretty quickly. You'll relieve a lot of stress and anxiety, and chances are that your body will function in a much better way. But that's not all, you'll also have a much better way of dealing with life, with all its twists and turns. This story sums up the essence of mindfulness in a beautiful way:

One day a student was out walking with his Zen master. The student suddenly stopped and asked the Zen master: "How can I reach enlightenment?"

The Zen master stopped and waited for a few seconds, before he answered: "Can you hear the babbling brook?"

Just as you learnt in the previous chapter, the ego will always try to reach, achieve or complete something. What the Zen master implied in his answer was that instead of being focused on reaching enlightenment, the student should be more focused on creating space between his thoughts. In other words, he should focus on becoming aware of the present moment.

Okay, so if the goal is to create space between our thoughts, how do we accomplish this? With all the things we have to do, with all the obligations of life. Wouldn't my life just fall apart, if I stopped thinking? Well let me invite you to consider the idea of repetitive thoughts. Some scientists claim that 95 to 99% of our thoughts are the precise same thoughts that we had the previous day. Don't you think some of these thoughts are a bit uninspired our outdated by now? By creating space through mindfulness, you can begin to bring in fresh and creative thoughts.

The Mindfulness Technique

Let's begin by covering the basics of the mindfulness technique. If you would rather learn this through video, then I deeply recommend the video from Jon Kabat-Zinn where he leads a mindfulness session at Google. In the end, he also answers some common questions that people might have, such as what to do if you fall asleep for example. If you want to watch the video, I'll have a link to YouTube where you can watch it. If you decide to watch it, just remember to come back to this book after your session is done. I have a lot more that I would like to share with you and that I think will benefit you in your life. The video can be found here: https://www.youtube.com/watch?v=3nwwKbM_vJc

Here is the mindfulness meditation technique:

Begin by finding a comfortable position to sit in. You can even choose to lie down if you want. However, if you have a tendency to fall asleep easily, then I recommend you sit. The only requirement here is that your body is in a position of dignity. So keep you back and neck straight. Look slightly down and close your eyes if you'd like. Closing your eyes is not a requirement, but since the eyes are like the door to our minds, I recommend you do it.

Become aware of your breath, both the inhale and exhale. Feel your nostrils, as the air you're breathing in is moving toward your lungs. Without changing anything, notice if you breathe with your stomach or chest.

Bring your attention back to your breathing whenever your mind wanders away. Be judgeless. In order words, don't beat yourself up if your mind wanders away a lot. If it wanders away a thousand times, you simply bring it back a thousand times.

When your mind is calm, begin to become aware of body as well. Begin with your toes and move upwards. Feel your legs, stomach, chest, neck, mouth, eyes and forehead.

When you're done, gently open your eyes and look around you. Keep the calm awareness. Perhaps you will feel a sense clarity when you see everything around you.

This is the essence of the mindfulness technique. There are no time requirements. You can do it for five minutes or five hours. My recommendation is that you do this daily. Even if you just do it for a few minutes. This is very powerful, especially if you begin your day with mindfulness, since the awareness of your whole day will be increased. Use the simple strategy of focusing on your breath to become present in the moment whenever you feel stressed or anxious.

Dealing with Unpleasant Thoughts

We are all looking for complex ways to understand how the world works. That's why we read books, attend seminars and look up to authorities. This is great, since it helps us to grow and improve or skills in different areas in our lives. However, sometimes we might already know or have the answer to some of life's dilemmas. But we don't act. It's as if we're saying to ourselves, "who am I to know?" When adopting mindfulness as a way of life, we begin to trust ourselves more. The intelligence inside of our mind and body is far greater than the ego paints it out to be. We just have to stop getting in our own ways. We have to stop the natural inclination to doubt ourselves. The only way we can accomplish this is through awareness. So in your everyday life, begin to become aware of your unpleasant thoughts. When you're more aware, you can easily change the thought pattern by simply letting the thought pass by. See the thought as a separate thing: "here it comes again". Don't judge it or invest emotion in it. Let it pass by as a cloud in the sky. Become aware of your body as well. If you're thinking unpleasant thoughts, you might have a tendency to frown, breathe shallower, or look down. When you become aware of this, free up you face, breathe into your stomach and look up as if you're the happiest person alive. Realize that your thoughts can't hurt you, only your response to them can.

Dealing with Unpleasant Emotions

The starting point for changing the unpleasant emotions in your life is to acknowledge them. This could be anger, stress, anxiety, or depression. Take time to reflect and examine how it feels. If you're stressed, perhaps you're feeling like you have a huge knot in your stomach. When you're angry, your muscles feel tight. If you're anxious, perhaps you feel a shortness of breath. If you're depressed, your energy is low and maybe your body feels stiff. By simply becoming aware, half the battle is won. The next step is to change the thoughts associated with these feelings. So instead of labeling it as anxiety, anger, stress, or depression, begin calling it a "sensation". It's neither good nor bad.

The final step is to act as if you're feeling the opposite of these emotions. You might say that's impossible. "You don't understand, these emotions take me over." If you had a gun pointed at your head, could you act despite these emotions? I bet you answered yes. So, if you feel the sensation of stress for example, don't judge it. Don't create a victim mentality around it by thinking about how bad it is. Acknowledge that it's there by bringing your awareness toward it. You're not afraid of this feeling, you are examining it with curiosity. Similar to step number 4 in the mindfulness technique, you bring your awareness through the whole body. Relax in the muscles that you find are tense and begin to breathe in a deeper way. Do this with every unpleasant emotion you might have. If you feel the sensation of depression, you might have to shake your body to relieve some suppressed energy. Think of a happy person and adopt the same posture as if you were happy. Your ability to deal with these emotions will drastically improve if you do this every time you experience an unpleasant emotion. Again, it all starts with your ability to bring awareness to whatever you want.

Worst Case Scenario

What if I lose my job? What if I fail? What if this (terrible thing) happen? Fear is one of the most destructive habits that we humans have. We fear the unknown and what might happen in the future. Instead of living in the present, we fear a future event that might never happen. Our ancestors probably had a lot fear about being eaten by a bigger animal. Perhaps they were also afraid of not having enough food. Maybe our habit of fear springs from their struggle to survive. However, the truth is that most of us have little real life and death situations to fear. Especially if you live in the Western world, you have it very good. According to globalissues.org, three billion people live on less than 2.5 dollars per day. That's almost half the world. Most of our fears are not grounded in reality and even if they are, why should we focus on it? It's not to say that you shouldn't be prepared if something were to happen, but obsessing about something that you can handle once it arises is not effective. Every minute you spend fearing the future, you lose one minute that you could have lived in the present moment. Reminding ourselves, from time to time, that we're all dying should not depress us. It should empower us.

So how do we break free from this prison called fear? Well, we have brought up the power of acceptance in chapter 2. The first step is to accept the fear. Do not try to fight it by wishing it that it could disappear. As a warrior of peace, we embrace the present moment, even if it contains an unwanted feeling. We then examine the fear by looking at it more closely. We feel the sensation in our body and figure out the thought associated with it. If it's a reoccurring fear, we write it down on a physical piece paper and try to figure out the roots of it. Once we have some kind of idea of the cause, we write down the worst possible thing that could happen if the fear came true. We do not try to fight the emotions that arise, we accept them. Now you should be able to see if your fear is grounded in reality or not. If it's not grounded in reality, then think of a voice that you can't take serious. It could be from a sitcom like **South Park**, or similar. Now imagine that voice saying your fear. "What if (fill in the blank)" After you've done it a couple of times in your head, either destroy the paper or throw it away to a corner. If the fear were to come again, simply apply the funny voice to it and deal with it in a similar way to how you learned to deal with an unpleasant thought.

On the other hand, if you think the fear is somewhat grounded in reality, the process is different. Let's say you wanted to start your own business, but were afraid to fail. Ask yourself a couple of questions after you have defined your worst case scenario. Answer these questions by writing them down.

1. What actions could you take to repair the damage if this were to happen?
2. What benefits can you find from this thing happening?
3. What action steps are you putting off out of fear?
4. Evaluate the downside of putting off this action step, what does it cost you?
5. What are you waiting for?

In the next chapter, we'll dive a little bit deeper into the subject of acceptance.

Chapter 16: Track Your Success And Improve Your Technique

The goal of this book is not merely to outline the theory of mindfulness. It is meant to immerse you in its practice and to show you how to embrace it and have it become your default mechanism so you can maintain a core of peace within despite your environment. Mindfulness is often overlooked because of how simple and straightforward it is in practice. You can take the tips and strategies that you have learnt here and begin to apply them immediately in formal meditation sessions or informally as you go about your daily life. If you are committed to being present in every moment then you will see the results.

The ultimate goal is to accept your emotions, yet become less reactive. Through practice you will learn how to recognize the negative emotions without being critical. Mindfulness demands that you show compassion to yourself first, then to others. Avoid judging. Allow your feelings and emotions to come to the surface of your mind, acknowledge them but choose your words and actions independent of them. This is true self-control.

Be consistent in the practice of mindfulness. Persistence is the key. As with anything new, it may be challenging at first but with practice, you will master it. One way of coming back to mindfulness time after time is to create triggers that will immediately remind you. Mindfulness triggers can be a particular action or event. Make it something that you do naturally and it immediately ushers you into a period of mindfulness. Examples may be whenever you sit for your evening meal, start your nightly bedtime ritual or even whenever you come to a red light. By association you would remember to be fully present in that moment.

Be kind to yourself at every stage and remember to acknowledge and celebrate your successes. You know the particular areas in which you want to regain control – I encourage you to write them down and from the techniques you have learnt here, create your own action plan. This has been said before but bears repeating, so at the risk of sounding trite - personalization leads to optimization.

Adopt mindfulness in all areas of your life. If you are eating a meal, be mindful about it. Resist catching up on the day's news while you eat. Instead bring your complete awareness to this one task. If you feel any restlessness when you make the decision, stop yourself and focus on the present. Close your eyes for a moment and observe your breathing and remind yourself about your commitment to be mindful 'I am being mindful of my eating', 'I will taste and enjoy every morsel of my meal'. We have been so programmed to multi-tasking that this is not as easy as it may sound. You may need to release yourself from any guilt you feel for 'wasting' time. Feel a sense of freedom to devote yourself wholly to your one task.

Practice the art of informal mindfulness throughout the day in simple tasks which are usually a routine. Keep a record of your successes. Make note of how many times you succeed at completing tasks mindfully and allow this to encourage you to make this a lifestyle change.

Learning to bring about a balance between relaxation and alertness is like fine tuning a guitar. You have to tread that fine line between them both. If you get so relaxed during mindful meditation that you feel the urge to doze, you are too relaxed. That is when you need to restore balance with mental alertness.

No matter where you are right now, bad relationships, stress-induced ill-health, depression, co-dependency, addictions – you can turn your life around. A holistic approach includes proper diet, nutrition, exercise and rest. Pay attention to each of these so that it supplements your practice of mindfulness. Take time out to do the things that you enjoy and spend quality time with the people who are important to you. Being present in each moment is being present for your life – do not miss that.

Chapter 17: Take Care Of Yourself

The habits that surround your life are more important than you think. All of the normal human activities have a purpose. Let's look at these in detail because you need to embrace habits that help you to make the most of your life.

Change Nutritional Habits

Earlier in the book, we talked about family meals, but we didn't tell you the full story. When you make unhealthy choices, what you do is set yourself up for guilt. Guilt eats away at your mind and makes you dislike yourself even more and isn't going to help self-love. People argue that good foods are more expensive, but if you total up what you spent on convenience foods in a week, you will find that you can buy the fresh equivalent for much less and although you need to do the cooking, you can make this a joint effort with your partner and turn it into an event. Be mindful of what you put into your body because what you get out of it will depend upon healthy nutrition.

Sleep like a baby

Something that stops us from sleeping is often the worries that go through our minds, but there may be other reasons why you are not getting the 8 hours that you need. Do you keep a window open in the bedroom? Is the temperature in your bedroom comfortable? Do you use nice clean cotton sheets? Do you sit up and watch violent movies late at night? Do you take all of your gadgets into the bedroom with you? You need to understand that most of the healing that goes on within the body depends upon sleep. Eating too soon before bedtime is also something you can change. Try to maximize your sleep hours so that your body is able to go through all of the changes it was designed to. Put away your mobile phone. Let go of worries and if you still find it hard to sleep, meditate before bedtime and put all of your worries out of your mind so that your mind is ready for sleep.

Chapter 18: My Experience Of Life

You now have all the tools you need to literally access the ground floor of experience. For me, after using the technique over and over, I realized how much I had missed out on the experience of life because my constant compulsive thinking was a barrier to my experience of life.

When you rely on your thinking mind, it tends to pull up the past. So in a way, you never actually experience what's right in front of you because your mind is always humming away.

Now that you know how to deal with that skillfully, you can turn off thinking and get back to experiencing. Eventually, you can disappear and melt into the experience completely. That is a topic we explore more in the next book.

Right now, your goal is to get some formal meditation in every day so you become familiar with the system. Once you can note without thinking about it, move on to adding it to other aspects of your life. Eventually, the goal should be to infuse every activity with mindfulness.

After I finsh this chapter, I'm going to take my dog for a walk. She's sitting by my feet waiting patiently. While we're walking, I start off slow, noting the movement of my legs. This will tell my mind I want to get into a my already conditioned-for, concentrated state. Then we will walk through the woods and enjoy the basic sensations of moving, touching, seeing, hearing, feeling. We will see trees and leaves and deer but when the mind tries to jump in and start labeling everything we will note it away until we're left with bare sensations.

Earlier, I said that there is a pleasurable body sensation that rises when we are concentrated. Over time, you will develop a simple joy that comes with just experiencing the senses. The whole world seems a little brighter and clearer without the fog of the mind. If given the choice between thinking about a thing and experiencing a thing, choose experience. If thoughts come up, you can look at them and watch them disappear. Or you can note them away.

There may be times when a memory or an important thought pops up during formal meditation. Make a note of it and analyze it after your session. It's important to focus on the experience while practicing and not what the mind wants to make the experience mean. Don't fall into the trap of psychoanalyzing on the cushion. It will slow down and hinder your practice.

I want you to set some goals for yourself now. You want to build the habit with meditation, but you need to spend enough time in one session practicing to make it worthwhile. In the beginning, I wouldn't do less than 30 minutes a day. You can do it in the morning (probably the best time) or at night. If you can do it after an exercise session, it's great. You have a lot of good-feeling body sensations to focus on making the practice pleasurable.

Although I said 30 minutes a day is good, if you can get in an hour a day it's even better. The practice needs some momentum to build-up. The good thing is, the more you practice the correct way, the more you will want to practice. We want to get to the point where you are using mindful awareness throughout the majority of your day. Remember our talk about conditioning? You will not get much benefit from spending 30 minutes being mindfully aware out of the 16 hours you are awake and having scattered attention. You're simply conditioning more of what you don't want.

The sooner you start practicing, the sooner you'll see benefits in other areas of your life.

I avoided the noting technique for quite some time because it seemed counterintuitive. It didn't seem like thinking all the time (noting) would be relaxing or a successful means of meditation. I was wrong and don't want you to make the same mistake.

If you really want all the benefits I've alluded to, you have to take this pretty serious. We have to overwrite or alter years and years of conditioning. The antidote to this is basically doing the technique correctly and for regular periods of time till it becomes your new default.

Try a 30 day challenge and practice for at least an hour a day formally. By formal, I mean either sitting or walking. You'll want a good base before the next book, where we'll talk about really deepening the practice.

After you have that 30 day base, start to apply it to your daily routine. Those 30 days will build up enough momentum and concentration power to get the benefits of incorporating it into everyday life.

I advise reading over the first few chapters a few times so you have a feel for them. Get the practice down first in your head so you have confidence when you're practicing. I suffered in the beginning because I was always worried I was practicing incorrectly. Use concentration, sensory clarity and equanimity as your guides. If those are present in ever-growing levels, then you're doing it right.

When you note, don't shout the label in your head. Say it softly and remember your focus should be on the thing you're noting, not the mental label.

If you're having a hard time focusing in the beginning, you can note out loud. Sometimes, the speaking of the label and hearing the label are what is needed to help block out a particularly noisy mind. This journey, like many others is about progress, not perfection.

My goal in this book has been to make you into a more mindful person who can bring a high level of concentration and equanimity to everything they do in life. The more present you are, the more you will enjoy your life, your family and your friends. The better equipped you'll be to treat people with compassion and equanimity. The better chance you'll have at making a difference in the world and making it a better place.

I hope you enjoyed this book and sincerely hope it serves you well.

Remember, when in doubt, note it out!

Chapter 19: What Is Mindfulness?

Have you ever started munching from a pack of chips, only to notice a little later that all you had was an empty packet? Or have you ever driven to a particular destination and realized that you are unable to recollect the path you travelled? You are not alone in this boat. It is pretty common and classic illustrations of "going on an autopilot" mode. Or, in simple words, being mindless.

We all have busy, hectic schedules, where we keep moving from one task to the next as if we have already been programmed. There is a set routine which we all rely on, and the slightest deviation from this comfort zone would invite undesirable anxiety, stress and worries. In the process, it is pretty easy to become or lose track of the present moment.

Human minds are easily distracted, habitually reliving the past moments and worrying about the unknown future. As I quoted in the beginning, whatever we experience today are results of our yesterday's thoughts and the thoughts we are dwelling on today will weave our future. Becoming more aware of our thoughts, feelings and sensations will help us let go of the past and future and think about the present, thus ensuring that we are being what we ought to be.

According to Jon Kabat-Zinn, "mindfulness means paying attention in a particular way; on purpose, in the present moment and non-judgmentally." It is a meditative state — a state where we are fully present in this moment — a heightened state of awareness that is free from any and all kinds of judgement, criticisms and worries. In this state, our minds are completely empty. There exists nothing but pure silence, yet we will be highly aware of whatever is happening within us and around us. But nothing affects us! In simple words, it is the state of pure bliss, joy and contentment.

"Mindfulness can simply be noticing what we don't normally notice, because our heads are too busy in the future or in the past - thinking about what we need to do, or going over what we have done."

Our mind is always filled with those unwanted and unpleasant thoughts that do not serve us in any way. And, therefore, mindfulness might seem to be a mountainous task. We are the masters of our minds and not vice versa. Hence, everything is in our hands.

Though it has its roots in Buddhist meditation, it has now become a secular thought which involves "maintaining a moment-by-moment awareness of our thoughts, feelings, bodily sensations and surrounding environment." Practicing mindfulness will help us tune into our sensations about the present rather than living in our past or imagining our future.

"What matters is to live in the present, live now, for every moment is now. It is your thoughts and acts of the moment that create your future. The outline of your future path already exists, for you created its pattern by your past, "said Sai Baba, a leading spiritual Guru from India.

The purpose of this book is to simplify your journey of regaining control of your thoughts and emotions. You don't need to be a monk and live in a mountain monastery or cave to get started. You don't even need a master. You can practice it here and now, even when you are bound by a busy schedule. The methods and tips described in the book are not time-consuming and can be easily integrated into your life, but to see results **you need to practice.**

Welcome to the world of mindfulness! Let's now create a new world for us!

Chapter 20: Harnessing The Present

The main problem with our modern world that plagues people is compulsive thinking. Most have a voice inside their head that is hysterically and constantly leaping from one thought to another, and never rests. The voice obsesses over any mistakes made, complains, compares, and loves to criticize everyone and everything. Most people are hostages to their own mind's whims, without even realizing that the mind is something separate from them, and not their entire identity.

You are not your Thoughts:

People mistakenly identify with the voice in their head, and their mind in general, without ever stopping to realize that their thoughts are not who they are. In fact, your thoughts are just a tiny piece of who you are, and you are the awareness that witnesses those thoughts. Think about it, when your mind is quiet, do you cease to exist? You are still there, and that you that exists in the silence, is the true you. As soon as you begin to observe the patterns of your thoughts and manage to refrain from mistaking them for you or judging them, you can enter into your truer nature, beyond your mind, and enter a state of happiness, joy, and peace.

How this Book will Help you:

This guide was created to tell you about a solution that allows you to live, peacefully, in the now. The now is the only moment that really exists, even though our minds love to try to convince us otherwise and hold us hostage in the past or future. Although the majority of people dwell in the phantoms of the past or future, there is an alternative. Mindfulness will allow you to immerse yourself in the experiences happening right now.

Harnessing the Present:

Salvation lies in harnessing the present and living in the now. This becomes easier once you realize that the present is the only real moment, and that the rest of your thoughts are simply illusory.

The Downfall of the Human Mind: How often do you notice that you are thinking about your past, regretting what you did, wishing things had happened differently? How often have you found yourself obsessing about what is yet to happen in the future, never even pausing to notice the accomplishments you are making in the present? All of us have been guilty of doing this. Actually, it gets even more intense when we find ourselves in stressful situations.

The Illusion of Control: The mind loves to feel as though it has control over situations, even though most of the time, it doesn't. This obsessive tendency to think over thoughts again and again and relive the past, and obsess over what hasn't happened yet, gives us the illusion that we are doing something about our unhappiness.

The present moment is not something special reserved for certain people, although many successful figures have found and utilized it. Anyone can do this. It's free, and it's your birthright as a human being. The moment you start celebrating the now, and shift your focus to existing instead of constantly seeking or obsessing, you become free.

Methods for getting Into the Now:

Many methods exist for entering the present moment and simply live in the now, and it's a highly personal process that you should be creative with. However, there are some techniques that will be helpful to beginners.

Positivity: Getting into the habit of shifting your focus to positive subjects will help you stay present. You can do this countless times during your daily activities. Some ideas to get you started are focusing on tiny accomplishments you may have mastered lately, thoughts that make you feel glad or excited, or simply focusing in on the positive attitudes of other people. All of those activities are useful for clearing the mind and zoning in on the present.

Journaling: In addition to positivity, you can access the now by recording and thinking about questions that allow you to feel the present. In the morning, come up with some specific questions that will help you remember to stay present, and at the end of the day, go over how well you did in your journal.

Questions to Ask Yourself for Presentness:

What strengths of mine can I focus on today?

What happened today that I can be grateful for?

What am I most proud of?

How can I live fully today?

Of course, having an idea of what your future will be like, and learning from your past is important to grow as a human being. But it's too easy to get caught up in this and completely distracted from life as it happens around us. Pausing to shift your mind to the present gives you power to continue moving forward, instead of getting stuck in this tempting trap of the mind. For this reason, you should begin today harnessing the present using discovery of the self. The past cannot be changed and the future cannot be predicted. The only control you have is right here in the present moment, so make the most of it!

Chapter 21: Understanding Mindfulness

There are a few things you need to understand first before moving on to the cream of this book. To engage in effective mindfulness practices, after all, means to fully grasp its origins and the reality of your life.

The Origin and Philosophy behind Mindfulness

The practice of mindfulness originated in Buddhism. According to their philosophy, **stress is caused by the emotions gripping a person's heart upon the arousal events**. These emotions are triggered by past memories or by judgment.

For example, the sight of a dirty homeless man can set a flurry of panic and worry. If the person really did have a bad experience with one, he or she has reason to feel that way. Because of mass media and stereotyping, however, even if there are no bad memories to associate the image, people automatically assume the homeless man should be dreaded, even if he is actually as harmless as a butterfly.

Regular people may find the above example a bit demeaning. It's the truth; people are (at relative degrees) judgmental. But it is also normal. Remembering or judging whether a thing, person or event is good or bad is every sane person's innate reflex. Humans, after all, are fragile. Man is designed to feel pain, fall ill, grow old and, of course, die. So far, being judgmental can and has saved numerous people from physical, emotional and mental harm.

Every sword meant to protect, however, also has the capacity to hurt its wielder. In the case of being judgmental, it can send anyone to a never-ending chain of worry, anxiety and stress. If left untamed, these three can quickly rob anyone of happiness, leaving nothing but suffering.

Now, during the olden days, the above explained process was yet to be understood. All people could do back then was feel the suffering. Instead of rationalizing and finding the root cause of it, however, they searched for salvation. Somehow, religions gave them what they needed. That was, of course, until Buddhism came along.

Understand that Buddhism is a philosophy, and not a faith or a religion. Buddha had never been a god, nor had he been the son of a god. He was as human as you. What made him god-like, however, was the fact that he had reached enlightenment -- the highest state of awareness man can achieve.

FYI: Anybody can reach enlightenment, and those who have were given the title Buddha. Gautama Buddha, the one everyone knows, was specially revered because he was the first man to have attained enlightenment, and he was every Buddhist follower's ultimate teacher.

What happens when you reach the highest state of awareness? It was said that not only will you be alleviated from suffering, you shall also gain perfect knowledge and wisdom.

According to Buddha's teachings, men are bound to suffer. It is what it means to be human after all. This also means that even if your neighbor or Facebook friend seems to be living the perfect life, he or she actually isn't.

Buddha also said there is a way to lift oneself from this suffering. Unlike the typical religion inviting people to cling to the belief that paradise awaits in the afterlife, however, Buddhism encourages followers to take control of the present -- to reign in their hearts and minds. Suffering is a state of mind, after all. Therefore, to change one's life means to change how one views it. And among the eight mental disciplines every Buddhist follower needs to harbor is mindfulness.

What It Means to Be Mindful

Just to be clear, mindfulness does not mean being mindful of others, or worrying whether you are positively appealing to them or not. In fact, this kind of mindfulness will require you to detach yourself from such thoughts.

Being mindful in this book's context means living and experiencing the present without judgement. Following the previous example, the sight of a homeless man should be nothing but the sight of a homeless man. No label of whether he is good or bad should accompany his image.

In other instances, being mindful simply means savoring the moment whether you are working on a report, washing the dishes, babysitting the kids, watering the garden, walking or driving to the supermarket, everything. This is probably the more important aspect of mindfulness. The current reality for most people, however, is the opposite.

When you brush your teeth, you think of several things (work, family, dinner, the laundry, an upcoming vacation, your ex, etc.) but not the act of brushing itself. What is there to mind in it after all? You've brushed a million times before, and your hands and arms shouldn't already need assistance. The very reason why humans developed muscle memory in the first place was to free enough brain space to accommodate another more important task.

Another good example is the long commute from home to work and vice versa. Instead of consuming the image of the grimy subway car or objectively observing the people inside it, everyone would rather put on their earphones and live inside their own world. Again, their heads are occupied by everything except the ride itself.

What is wrong with these examples? It may sound ridiculous, but the thoughts that captivate you during these events are actually the roots of worry, anxiety and stress as discussed in the previous topic.

Most people are not aware of it, but they instinctively attach emotions to objects, places or events. The workplace, for example, is in most cases equivalent to a torture chamber. Therefore, when a person is reminded of unfinished tasks at work during his peaceful train ride home, he would feel worry. Apparently, however, emotions do not always end with worry. Anxiety often follows, and in the case of the given example, the brain could begin anticipating an angry boss the next day.

And since the person cannot do anything about his unfinished task because he's helplessly standing in the middle of a long train ride, he will inevitably feel more stressed.

Now, in the simplest term, all that is unnecessary. There is nothing the person could have done in the first place except worry, so there's no point in even thinking about it. But this is inevitable for an untrained mind -- one that is allowed to unconsciously drift everywhere.

Basically, this is what mindfulness seeks to correct. You will practice avoiding settling in any kind of thought. You will then pour your entire focus on the things you often disregard, like the lady sitting in front of you, reading the same book you love, or feeling the slight pinch of the cold winter air in your cheeks. In summary, mindfulness will teach you to live in the present. the goal in this slight change of focus is to bring you inner peace.

Chapter 22: What Is The Practice Of Mindfulness?

A simple definition of mindfulness is: It is the ability of an individual to pay attention to what is happening in the present moment without being judgmental.

In this crazy world that is full of chaos and confusion, what you need to cope with all the craziness and retain a bit of happiness is the practice of mindfulness. Without this practice, you will find yourself losing connection with what is happening presently around you.

Mindfulness comes to you naturally, and it is ready for you to use in every moment of your life. You need to be prepared to appreciate its existence. It is like art which you can use to create a space for yourself to think, making space to breathe and the space needed for your reaction to things.

When you know how to control your thinking concerning the world around you or to focus on the present moment, it is the practice of mindfulness. You only need to pay attention to what you decide your focus should be and shielding the rest away.

If you find yourself in a position where you can view the world and your surroundings without being judgmental, you have arrived at the state of mindfulness. Accepting all that is happening around you as regular occurrences without judgment is the gateway to true happiness.

If you can learn how to practice mindfulness in your everyday living properly, you have the key to reduce anxiety, stress and time wasted while feeling overwhelmed.

The practice of mindfulness is what will enable you to appreciate and enjoy each moment as it occurs and to regard it as precious. You don't have to wallow in things of the past, worry about what will happen to you in the future, or concern yourself with reactions or judgments to the things you are seeing. Unknown to you, wallowing in all these worries are making you miss out on the essential things in life. You will be left with a shadow of yourself, unsettled in your mind, feeling empty and unsatisfied while what is in the present, what is now, slips away.

In a nutshell, the practice of mindfulness in your everyday life is like a psychological procedure which you can use to bring the attention of an individual to the experiences that are happening presently. For a person to reach this state of mind, you have to develop it and to go through the training processes.

How Does it Work

The workings of mindfulness will enable you to be aware of your feelings and thoughts more clearly.

It will:

☐ Make you aware of your usual reactions and events to the happenings around you

☐ Become aware of your thoughts and your experiences of the world

☐ Notice your response to your feelings and thoughts

☐ You will also realize when you are overwhelmed by negative thoughts and look for ways to change your thinking

The mindful practice aims to enable you to focus on the present events and to let go of the painful past.

It can only achieve this objective by working on certain aspects of your existence such as:

Autopilot

This state of mind is the time you are not attentive to what you are doing in your daily living. Although it is useful to operate on automatic pilot since you can complete every task easily, you can also mistakenly get caught by reactions and thoughts which are not helpful. That is the reason mindfulness encourages you to be extra attentive when carrying out your usual routine such as showering, eating or walking.

Being and doing mode

The being mode is a state of mind where you are happy and ready to accept your life the way you are without putting any pressure on yourself. On the other hand, the doing mode is the state of mind where you are ready to respond to the world around you. Although this mindset may help you to solve problems and reach your goals, it can leave behind anxiety and stress.

According to scientific findings, mindfulness practices work through the changes in our brain and our body's creation of hormones with other chemical substances that have an impact on our physical health.

Scientists are of the opinion that the advent of mindfulness can lead to non-reactive acceptance and non-judgmental experiences which is connected to physical and psychological results.

The practice of mindfulness begins from the following:

The Brain

A significant research finding in 2014 is of the opinion that the brain is in association with mindfulness practices. According to a brain imaging research, eight regions of the brain are consistently changed during mindfulness practice.

The regions altered are as follows:

☐ The Frontopolar Cortex- This part of the brain is in charge of your emotions, thoughts, and self-awareness.

☐ Insula and Sensory Cortices- This part of the brain takes care of your body awareness.

☐ The Hippocampus- This side takes care of all your memories.

☐ The Orbitofrontal Cortex, Mid, and Anterior cingulate-This particular part is incharge of regulating your emotions and self.

☐ Corpus Callosum and Upper Longitudinal Fasciculus- This part takes care of the communication between the brain and its components.

This finding is consistent with the research that follows how a person's perception changes according to their physiological measures and behaviors such as stress hormones, brain waves or activities. According to this research, mindfulness practice is associated with particular changes in the functional structure of the brain and also with the particular change in behavior. What it all boils down to is that mincful practice has an advantageous effect on a person's feelings and thoughts. It can also be a positive element in decreasing pain and fear.

During the mindful practice process, the part of the brain that is connected to the feelings of pain is disconnected from the prefrontal cortex which is where emotions are typically processed. This action results in the reduction of the emotional pain experience.

As for fear, scientists have used the FMRI which is a brain imaging device to show that you can calm fear with mindful practice. The findings from Harvard and Stanford university's researchers shows that mindfulness can reduce the rate of neurons and the activity of the amygdala which is a vital area that regulates emotions. As a result of this practice, the center of the brain that reacts to fear shrinks leaving room for the center for thoughtful response to grow.

In a nutshell, what this research is talking about is that mindful practice reduces the fearful and reactive instincts of an individual and increases the thoughtfulness of the individual's perception of events.

The Body

It is also essential to note that mindful practices also work through the body systems. It induces the response of relaxation in the body through the Parasympathetic nervous system. This system is in charge of restoring the base levels of your body as you pass through a stress response. It will reduce your muscle tension, blood pressure, respiratory and heart rate respectively.

Mindfulness practices can also cause a reduction in all the other physical manifestations of stress like Interleukin 6, Cortisol and C-reactive Proteins. This reduction action is vital since the physical symptoms of stress can lead to the increased risk of severe diseases like heart irregularities, digestive disorders, high blood pressure, insomnia, diabetes, persistent fatigue, mental health problems and reduced fertility if it persists.

Chapter 23: What Is Mindfulness?

I could arrange this book in such a way that you have to build up to mindfulness. I could talk about how bad for you stress is, or I could talk about neuroscience.

But I'll get to that later. What you probably want to know right off the bat is just what mindfulness is. Where did it come from? And how can you use it just to get a little more calm and relaxation in your life?

We'll look at that first and from there, we'll delve into how you can utilize some more technical neuroscience in order to tap into the more profound capabilities of your brain...

So what exactly is mindfulness?

Essentially, mindfulness is a form of meditation that has been adopted by CBT. CBT in turn is 'cognitive behavioral therapy'; a psychotherapeutic approach that can be used to treat all manner of psychological conditions like anxiety, phobias, addiction etc.

Mindfulness essentially gives us a tool that we can use to not only calm our thoughts and escape the stressors of the day but also reflect on the contents of our mind in the interests of self-improvement.

Meditation generally has something of a 'bad' reputation. That is to say that a lot of people associate it with religion or esoteric ideas and they think that they can't meditate unless they're 'spiritual'. This can be off-putting for someone who doesn't hold any religious beliefs or who doesn't like esoteric ideas in general.

But in fact you can practice meditation whether you are religious or an atheist. All meditation really is, is a directed attempt to control your thoughts and the content of your mind and thereby to gain some peace and quiet or at least to be able to better understand the contents of your own brain.

Often this means completely silencing all thoughts. Many types of meditation, such as transcendental meditation, instruct you to think of 'absolutely nothing' and often this is achieved by focussing on your breathing, a mantra or a physical object like a candle flame. This can be difficult for beginners though, as they constantly find their mind wandering.

The idea behind mindfulness meditation then is not to try and empty your thoughts but instead to simply step back from them and 'observe' them like a detached third party. This way, you aren't letting your thoughts affect you and make you stressed but you also aren't going to struggle with not being 'allowed' to think anything.

Meanwhile, using this technique will also allow you to become more aware of your own thoughts and thereby able to edit any thoughts that are leading you into trouble. For instance, if you constantly find yourself thinking about the ways that you could hurt yourself, you might notice that this is a bad habit and then attempt to fix that.

This may be the long term aim of mindfulness when used in CBT. In the short term though, we are simply to use it in order to remove ourselves from our thoughts and emotions so that we can get some calm and thereby recover ready to tackle the day ahead.

Mindfulness in Daily Life

This is what mindfulness refers to in most cases but it has also been appropriated to mean a lot more. If mindfulness means being more aware of your thoughts, then it can also be applied outside of meditation and to the way you go about your day. In this case, mindfulness simply means being mindful of what you're focussing on and what you're thinking at any given point. This is useful because very often you'll find that your mind isn't perhaps where it should be.

For example, if you are walking through a beautiful scenic woodland but you are thinking about work, then as far as your body is concerned you may as well be at work. In this case, mindfulness can be used simply to make yourself more aware of where you are and to actually focus on what's around you. That means feeling the breeze on your skin, looking at the beautiful flowers and smelling the fresh air. When you do all that, you will benefit much more from the experience.

Likewise, you can use mindfulness to direct your attention to all manner of other things. For example your physical sensations. Often we aren't aware of just how we're sitting, how we're standing or how we're feeling.

Take a moment right now to reflect on this. How comfortable are you at the moment? Does any part of your body hurt? If you're sitting down, then where is most pressure on you? Can you feel your clothes against your body? A watch maybe? How warm are you? Are you leaning more to one side?

This kind of mindfulness can be useful if you want to try and fix your posture but also if you want to improve your abilities in sports or just move more efficiently.

Being more mindful of the way you speak can meanwhile help you to speak more eloquently, to stop using derogatory words, to stop swearing, or to change the whole way that people perceive you. For example, if you want to sound more intelligent, then you can simply try using bigger words or speaking a little more slowly.

You can also use mindfulness to be happier in every day life. Simply try to stop letting negative emotions affect you by identifying them as temporary and destructive. You can simply 'notice' that you're getting angry and acknowledge that your thoughts will be tainted by that. With practice, this can make you a much calmer and much happier person.

But what do you find when you try and do this?

In all likelihood, you'll find that you forget. This is just the same way that you forget to pick up bread when your other half asks you to. And it's just the same way you forget to pick up your keys on the way out of the house.

The point is: most of the time we have no control over what we're focussed on or what we're paying attention to. And as such, we find ourselves forgetting things, getting into bad habits or stressing when we should be enjoying ourselves.

Practicing mindfulness both as a form of meditation and during the day can therefore help you to improve your ability to control your thoughts and thereby to decide how you want to improve yourself and what you want to focus on.

Chapter 24: What Is Meditation?

Human brain is in a constant state of unrest. Our five main senses are sight, sound, touch, taste and feeling. These senses confuse us and put us in a state of quandary. The disturbed mind is unable to think with clarity, retain pure thoughts or have a clean vision which tangles us up in knots of deep sorrow. Meditation acts as a mental exercise that helps us to remain calm and think clearly.

In today's world there is stress and strain everywhere. Be it in relationship or at your job, stress is unavoidable. Modern gadgets and our minute to minute lifestyle add to our stress factor majorly. People are looking for ways to relax and release their stress. That is why we see gyms and yoga studios up and about at every corner of the world. But no gym is good enough, your gym might help you to lose some weight and look glamorous but running on the treadmill in an air conditioned room alone does not provide one with a calm and tranquil mind. Working out your mind is much more important than pulling a few muscles. Freeing the mind from droning thoughts and everyday training is the main aim of meditation.

Man is a social animal and though we are at peace with ourselves for the first few years of our life, our daily interactions result in a worked up mess as we grow old. It is then that complaints, confusions and worries become second nature to us. And that is when we feel at a loss of harmony. I would like to assure you that peace has to be found from within and not from the outside world. The outside world has and shall never provide the serenity you wish for. It's from within that serenity must be found. Sit in a quiet place and look within yourself. When your senses are in a state of silence you'll feel the real peace.

Your mind is like a monkey. It flits from one craving to another trying to engorge the senses with the pleasures of the instant. When the mind is filled with distractions, how can it concentrate on one goal? The solution is to control the senses with the power of your mind. It is here that meditation helps. Sitting in a place for at least ten minutes a day concentrating on a single object can help you to keep calm and concentrate on a specific goal. Peace and tranquility are part and parcel of our mental makeup. It is there with us every single moment of our life. Only we don't recognize it. That is because we're ignorant about the calm when all along it is there right within us. We're so caught up with the external world that we forget to look within to find tranquility.

Being at peace with yourself is what matters and meditation helps you to achieve exactly that. Meditation has proved to be the best alternative therapy. Even doctors around the world recommend their patients to perform meditation to be free from worries.

You need two things to achieve freedom from stress and worry. A silent mind and an open heart!
Popular misconceptions about meditation

There is a popular misconception that meditation is a part of Hindu religion and because of it many people have lost a huge opportunity to derive benefits of this practice. I am saying it here once again for clarification – Meditation has nothing to do even remotely with any religion. By meditating you will not become a heathen. You can practice meditation even when following your religion. Meditation does not discriminate between a Christians, Muslims, Jews or any other form of religion. Perhaps the beauty of meditation lies in the fact that anyone and everyone can practice it without compromising on their religious beliefs.

The second misconception which keeps people away from meditation is that it's very tough and difficult. I have heard stories which claim that mediation means sitting in one posture for hours together. Another popular myth is that meditation means abstaining from the pleasures of life. There are absurd claims that meditation requires you to be celibate - not to have sex. Who would want to take up meditation if there are so many restrictions in practicing it?

Let me put the above misconceptions to rest. You don't have to it for hours in meditation. At the very most you may have to be still for thirty minutes. Meditation is not hard work or manual labor. There are no restrictions in having sex or enjoying the good life. It actually empowers you to enjoy life to the fullest. It enables you to be active, energetic and joyful. You are all fired up and ready to go after a session of mediation. Sometimes, meditation is compared to having drugs without the side effects. Practitioners of meditation have confessed to a greater level of awareness and a sense of everlasting happiness. It brings perspective to life and creates opportunities at a sub-conscious level.

Meditation is sometimes wrongly compared to black magic. I don't know where or how this concept originated, but I can tell you that it's utter rubbish. Meditation has nothing to do with magic — black, white or any other color.

I have mentioned many times that meditation is a spiritual practice. This may seem confusing to many readers. By spirituality, I mean that mediation is a practice to reach greater level of consciousness. This consciousness is universal and an inherent part of human condition regardless of their religion. Pure consciousness refers to a true understanding of our life. It's also called realization. Words life awareness, insight, vision are related to the concept of consciousness.

Now that you know about the facts of meditation, you can confidently embrace it and enjoy its true benefits.

Meditation is a way of life

Your body consists of flesh, blood and nervous system. Every part of your body must be in harmony if you want to achieve happiness and wellbeing. Meditation helps in reaching a state of wellbeing in which you are completely relaxed and find joy. There are many reasons why people practice meditation. Some take up meditation for relief from a temporary problem. There are people who want to discover their inner self. Spirituality is another goal which people pursue using meditation as a tool. You must have noticed that people have become health conscious. You can only have a healthy body if you have a healthy mind. Health problems are generally related to stress and worries. Meditation is a fantastic way to get rid of tension. There is only one way to achieve happiness. That is to simply be happy. You are probably thinking right now "How do I get to be happy? Things just don't work like that; it doesn't take into consideration the times that I am miserable because of problems or mishaps that come up in my everyday life, not to mention the tragedies." At this point you've to stop and meditate. Meditation can be done in many different ways, just identify the one that works best for your specific need.

Frankly, being happy is an incredibly difficult task to accomplish. This may look like a paradox. You want to achieve happiness and meditation seems to be a good way to achieve it but at the same time everyone admits that a happy state of mind is extremely difficult to achieve - Yet, I still say that meditation can lead to longer period of happiness. The path that you have chosen that led you to your current situation was not a few days or months in the making, but a long and strenuous path that has spanned through many years. This decision of starting a meditation practice has not happened of a sudden. I am sure that this thought has been on your mind for a long time. It is a fact that you start something only when the time has come for it. Maybe it's time for you to start meditating.

Think about it - In reality it has taken you as long as you have been alive to become the way you are today. It has also taken you that long to achieve what you have achieved, to possess and to arrive at your current condition. Take the time to meditate and think about whom you are and what you have in your life is truly what you want or not. If you are completely satisfied with the way your life is going, congratulations-do more of what you have been doing and you will get more of what you already have in your life. But if you're unhappy with your present situation and want to be different, then you have to start meditating and also make some basic changes to your life. Failure to make those changes will find yourself continue to seek the things you really would like in your life but without success. Some of what you are about to read will seem impossible, ridiculous to you or maybe even foolish. I urge you to give it a try. In this day and time with all the things we have to deal with in our lives, it is very hard to stay on a positive level and be happy all the time. By taking few minutes in a day just meditating will help you to keep things in right perspective, where instead of being unhappy about the situation you are in, you can find a way to happiness.

Mediation is a solitary practice but can also be conducted in a group. Many guided meditation techniques highlight the advantages of group meditation.

According to some meditation experts, group mediation leads to a collective consciousness which is much bigger than the sum total of individual consciousness. This is also called resonating energy. There is a scientific explanation for this phenomenon. Meditating in a group has other benefits as well. By discussing your individual progress with others you can resolve some issues faster than you could if you were alone. Group mediation is usually conducted by experts who can guide you through the process. This does not mean that you can't practice meditation on your own. You can meditate in a place of your choice and pick a suitable time without getting tied to a program. Mediation is a flexible practice. Meditation has been proved to heal mental diseases as well. Mediation can work wonders for patients suffering from mental disorders, if accompanied by suitable medication. You should not take medicines without consulting a physician. Many people may not be diagnosed with serious mental sickness but yet may suffer its debilitating effect. Many cases go unnoticed and undiagnosed. Meditation can be effective in avoiding escalation of mental illness.

Interestingly many physical ailments are related to our mind. It is scientifically proven that cardiac failures can occur because of sudden stress. Chronic headaches, belly ache and muscular pain are associated with the mental state. In such cases meditation is a viable solution. By de-stressing the mind and allowing free flow of energy, you can control if not totally eliminate physical distress. Meditation must become a way of life and a daily practice.

Essentially, meditation is a practice that helps to keep the mind still and stay calm. You can learn these techniques within a few minutes. Sit erect in a place and close your eyes. Try to concentrate on one single object or nothing. There ……. Now you have started your meditating session.

Conclusion

Since the time Jon Kabat Zinn became convinced that mindfulness can be of so much help, a lot of insight has been gained into the value of mindfulness. This eBook has contributed to the benefits of believers in the concept.

To maximize your benefit from mindfulness, take very good care to understand everything written here. Read in-between-the-lines to understand mindfulness in itself. Then, as you grow through the pages, ask yourself whether or not you need mindfulness due to the reasons why others need it. Do you remember the top 5 mindfulness practice we discussed? There's more to it, as you have probably seen while going through how mindfulness can boost your focus and while you were reading practical tips for managing negative emotions.

May all you have read here make you a mindful person.

www.ingramcontent.com/pod-product-compliance
Lightning Source LLC
Chambersburg PA
CBHW072002070526
44583CB00015B/1302